More Praise for *Wor*

"Sancken offers a timely vision of preaching as truth-telling. This deeply resourced yet accessible book offers tangible tools—from preparation to delivery—for transforming the way that the Christian gospel meets the lives of persons of faith. Seeking to form 'trauma-aware' preachers, Sancken may find herself leading a new movement in contemporary preaching."

—Shelly Rambo, associate professor of theology, Boston University School of Theology, Boston, MA

"At the heart of the Christian gospel is the wounded heart of God in the shape of the cross of Jesus Christ. Professor Joni Sancken ushers readers into the presence of this wounded God and wounded world, not to inflict more hurt but for the purpose of leading others toward healing through the preaching of a cruciform Word. Through theological, biblical, and practical guidance, Sancken provides soul words for soul wounds. This book is a balm from God!"

—Luke A. Powery, dean, Duke University Chapel; associate professor of homiletics, Duke Divinity School, Duke University, Durham, NC

"Joni Sancken brings together a deep love for the gospel with a deep heart for the traumatized in these pages. Pastors struggling to find the right word for a wounded people in many difficult seasons will find great help in her company."

—David Schnasa Jacobsen, professor of the practice of homiletics; director, Homiletical Theology Project, Boston University School of Theology, Boston, MA

"Trauma comes in so many forms to individuals and communities today. A person in the prime of life drops dead. A soldier is immobilized by the thought, 'I killed someone.' Natural disaster, economic collapse, political repression. Joni Sancken helps preachers identify biblical, theological, historical, and pastoral resources to address the spectrum of situations of trauma so that congregations have the opportunity to engage the gospel with its reassurance, guidance, and challenge."

—Ronald J. Allen, professor emeritus of preaching and Gospels and Letters, Christian Theological Seminary, Indianapolis, IN

Other Books in the Artistry of Preaching Series

Preaching as Poetry: Beauty, Goodness, and Truth in Every Sermon
by Paul Scott Wilson

Actuality: Real Life Stories for Sermons That Matter
by Scott Hoezee

Preaching in Pictures: Using Images for Sermons That Connect
by Peter Jonker

Preaching with Empathy: Crafting Sermons in a Callous Culture
by Lenny Luchetti

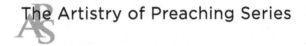The Artistry of Preaching Series

Words That Heal

Preaching Hope to
Wounded Souls

Joni S. Sancken

Abingdon Press
Nashville

WORDS THAT HEAL:
PREACHING HOPE TO WOUNDED SOULS

Copyright © 2019 by Abingdon Press

All rights reserved.

This book is printed on acid-free paper.

Library of Congress Cataloging-in-Publication Data has been requested.

978-1-5018-4968-8

19 20 21 22 23 24 25 26 27 28—10 9 8 7 6 5 4 3 2 1
MANUFACTURED IN THE UNITED STATES OF AMERICA

Contents

Series Preface

The Artistry of Preaching series gives practical guidance on matters that receive insufficient attention in preaching literature yet are key for preachers who seek greater creative expression in their preaching. Fresh, faithful proclamation requires imagination and creative engagement of the Bible and our world. There is no shortage of commentaries on the Bible and books on biblical interpretation for preaching, but there is a shortage of practical resources to help strengthen the creativity of preachers to facilitate their proclamation of the gospel.

The first volume of this series, *Preaching as Poetry: Beauty, Goodness, and Truth in Every Sermon*, redefines preaching for our current postmodern age. The world has changed. Beauty, goodness, and truth no longer mean what they used to mean as fixed absolute and universal standards. While this may be threatening to some preachers, the new meanings can actually allow preachers fresh and creative ways to proclaim God's love and saving purposes in a rapidly changing world. Preaching needs to be reconceived as a kind of poetry, in the sense of communicating the wondrous beauty of God's saving purposes and promises in troubled times. God needs to be presented in terms of experience and relationships, more than abstractions, and faith needs to be presented as something that adds beauty, goodness, and truth to life. In other words, for a new generation that seeks concrete outcomes and immediate benefits, faith needs to be presented as a relationship with God and neighbor that affords deep meaning and great joy.

The second volume of the series, *Actuality: Real-Life Stories for Sermons That Matter*, by Scott Hoezee, is a resource for preachers who want guidance to be better storytellers or to use story more effectively to communicate with a new generation. There readers will also find a collection of stories that both preach and stimulate their imaginations to identify stories from their own contexts. Preachers can easily run out of good stories to use that embody the gospel. The problem is not a shortage of stories; they are all around in everyday events. The task is learning how to harvest them, as will be shown here. Preachers long for good stories, and today's listeners are not content with the canned internet illustrations that sound artificial and have a predictable moral. Rather they want stories rooted in the actual world in which they live, that depict life as they know it, and that can function as Jesus's stories did, as parables and metaphors that bear God's grace to their hearers.

The third volume, *Preaching in Pictures: Using Images for Sermons That Connect*, helps preachers add some spark and imagination with a dominant or captivating image. The challenge is not just to find images that are visually evocative; it is to find ones that are artistic, propulsive, and theologically centered. By moving from a theme sentence to an image statement, preachers can move their composition from being a "beautiful mess" to an affective sermon. Preachers can benefit from the book's practical exercises adapted from creative writers and poets that help in the art of selecting images and polishing them for use in relation to biblical texts. Equally important in the current times, readers will find guidance on using images on screens in worship that can powerfully assist the work of the Spirit and increase the joy of preaching.

The fourth volume of The Artistry of Preaching series is *Preaching with Empathy: Crafting Sermons in a Callous Culture* by Lenny Luchetti. Empathy is a subject that some people might not connect with art and artistry. They may think of empathy as a feature of personality, something one either has or does not have. To some degree, they are right. What makes the present volume so remarkable is that Lenny Luchetti teaches the art of putting empathy into practice in preaching. However great or small our natural empathy, it can be enhanced by tending to it.

Empathy is needed for preaching to be transformative for the listeners and society in general. It is not enough for preachers just to know they love their congregations. The congregations must know it. Preachers must show it, ensuring that it is experienced through what is done and said. Empathy must be nurtured and communicated through what one says about the Bible and the world today, and about the various relationships fostered in preaching. While the preacher's love for the people is essential, the goal of empathic homiletical practice is to communicate God's love in Christ and through the Spirit, to enable the people's ministry through empathy for one another. In other words, empathy is a spiritual practice that individual preachers can cultivate and utilize to enhance their sermons, as Luchetti shows and as many have done through history. His volume could not come at a better time, when so much in the current culture seems to point toward apathy. He brings a corrective that is hopeful, practical, encouraging, and inspiring.

Words That Heal: Preaching Hope to Wounded Souls is the fifth volume of the series. In this innovative volume, Joni Sancken develops tools for preachers to speak effectively to people in congregations who carry with them the effects of untended wounds caused by past hurts, brokenness, tragedies, and trauma. These include the effects of sexual or emotional abuse, witnessing violence perhaps in war, or having caused an accident or hurting someone you love. Wounds to the soul, if ignored, can be debilitating and inhibit growth. This volume teaches that there is an art to ministering to soul wounds. Together with the Holy Spirit, preachers can initiate and help participate in a healing process. Not everyone in the pews has suffered trauma, but everyone carries pain. Everyone can benefit from hearing issues named, the truth spoken in love, and words that offer hope. Sancken offers practical tools. She encourages preachers to proclaim what the church uniquely offers: the love, healing grace, and redemptive power of God that emanates from the cross of Christ. This book is about compassionate preaching that not only heals but also restores faithful and joyous community.

The aim of the series is to be practical, to provide concrete guidelines and exercises for preachers to follow, and to assist them in engaging practices. Preaching is much more than art, yet by ensuring that we as preachers employ artistry in our preaching, we assist the Holy Spirit in communicating the gospel to a new generation of people seeking God.

—Paul Scott Wilson, Series Editor

Acknowledgments

There are many people to thank for their help and support. Through the Homiletical Theology Project, David Jacobsen and Andre Resner gave me helpful feedback on an essay that served as a seed for this project. Mary Thiessen Nation and my fellow learners in the Strategies for Trauma Awareness and Resilience (STAR) training in February 2017 introduced me to key writers and theories. Ron Allen, Tom Dozeman, and Andrew Park championed this project and encouraged me to pursue publication. Paul Scott Wilson and Connie Stella believed in this project and offered support and help along the way. The faculty development committee, Academic Dean David Watson, President Kent Millard, and the Board of Trustees at United Theological Seminary granted me a sabbatical to write this book. I am also thankful for my faculty colleagues at United who offered feedback and for the skillful editing work of Chad Clark.

This project benefited from the input of others who are on a journey to healing or accompanying others toward healing. I am thankful to the many people who shared their experiences and stories with me. Our conversations unfolded on holy ground. I also thank the pastors and students who willingly shared their sermons with me, particularly Bob Howard, whose sermons nourish my faith and sense of hope for the church.

I would not have been able to write this book without my family. I thank my husband, Steve, and children, Maggie and Teddy, for their patience, support, and love. Finishing this book was truly a family effort! I thank my mom, Lynne Sancken, for providing childcare while I took STAR training. I also thank my extended Schumm family for allowing me to share our experience of my sister-in-law Twila Tonelli's death. This book is dedicated to her.

Introduction

On July 4, 2016, my sister-in-law died from a brain aneurysm. She was a healthy young mom with a baby and a preschooler. Her death was sudden and traumatic for our whole family. After this heartbreaking experience, I became more attuned to the wounds that other families and individuals carry and how these wounds can affect relationships with God and the church. Those who write about healing from trauma often have a personal catalyst. Our family's journey through trauma toward healing is traced in these pages.

Several concerns lie at the heart of this book: (1) Many pastors lack knowledge and in-depth awareness of trauma and the unseen wounds created by traumatic experience. Some pastors are afraid to acknowledge these wounds out of fear of stirring up old pain. (2) Often preachers turn to psychological or therapeutic language to minister to those with soul wounds. I want to encourage robust theological engagement that harnesses preaching to connect experiences that wound us and claims that lie at the heart of the gospel. (3) Because many people who survive trauma experience shame and isolation, I want to empower preaching that nurtures those who have experienced trauma and participates in God's healing and restoration.

This book equips preachers to help individuals and congregations heal from traumatic experiences and develop resilience. Church members can carry many types of relational and psychological wounds. Trauma refers specifically to circumstances in which a person survives a life-threatening experience or loses a loved one suddenly, where one's ability to process experience is surpassed by the breadth or depth of the experience itself. However, this book will also be helpful for preachers seeking to facilitate God's healing for other experiences of pain and brokenness that fall short of trauma but still cause harm. I use the term *soul wounds* to refer to unattended and unhealed effects of trauma and other pain that impact individuals and communities physically, emotionally, mentally, relationally, sociologically, and spiritually.

Resilience is the ability of a person or group to withstand, adapt, and in some sense bounce back following an experience of trauma or adversity. Resilience is a gift of God's grace that preachers can cultivate as part of congregational formation for participation in a wide range of ministries.

Chapter 1 will discuss the origins and characteristics of soul wounds, providing definitions and theories associated with the field of trauma studies to help preachers recognize symptoms of unaddressed traumatic experience. It will show how the church can utilize some therapeutic approaches alongside theological frameworks. Trauma awareness can help pastors preach relevant and restorative sermons to those who have experienced trauma and others with unhealed wounds from a range of past hurts.

Chapter 2 will highlight the effects of trauma in and behind the Bible. The first part of the chapter lifts up five interpretive tools for preachers. The second part demonstrates these tools as part of a process for moving from biblical text to sermon.

Chapter 3 will address the church's role in causing or intensifying traumatic wounds, using sexual abuse in the church as a case study and example to discuss dynamics present with a broader range of wounds and situations. I discuss resistance to addressing wounds in the church and aspects of the wound of sexual abuse before offering preachers suggestions that can foster healing. A sample sermon demonstrates the techniques discussed.

Chapter 4 is focused on approaches to preaching that can foster God's healing for trauma or other situations of brokenness. The chapter begins with a discussion of how preaching can deepen listeners' experience of the gospel and nurture congregational resilience. Then, I extend an array of possible approaches and examples including preaching in the immediate aftermath of a wounding event and moving outward toward preaching as a means of healing and broader Christian formation exemplified by a sermon series focused on preaching through the Apostle's Creed to form listeners according to the life of Christ. Listeners who are deeply formed according to the life of Christ are equipped with theological faith tools to face life and minister to others in a wounding world.

In the resurrection of Jesus Christ, Christians have access to hope beyond the realm of what is possible for us by ourselves. In the wake of wounding experiences, many may be moved to cry or pray. Others simply feel numb. Numbness keeps us passive and unengaged in the pain of others. It masks the wounds that we ourselves carry and robs us of hope—hope that is in short supply in many parts of our world today.

This book encourages preachers to be proactive about nurturing hope and healing in our congregations and communities and to bear witness to God's healing actions and intentions in our world. As preachers and Christian leaders, we join a chorus of other witnesses across time as proclaimers of the healing presence of Christ who takes our own wounds into the wounded heart of God and transforms our lives for God's glory.

Chapter 1
Soul Wounds

Human responses to traumatic or wounding experiences are mysterious. We do not understand why some people emerge seemingly unscathed in the wake of horrific events while others remain wounded and are unable to return to meaningful life and relationships. Consider these scenarios.

- A parenting group meets in a church basement. A few women linger afterward to share stories of childbirth. Some of the mothers express feelings of grief, shame, and isolation at what they expected to be a joyful time. Their experiences of birth were not positive but rather were experiences of deep fear or powerlessness.

- A man in his mid-thirties doesn't drive. He has arranged his life around walking and taking public transportation. When he was a teenager, he lost both parents in a fatal car accident and has been unable to get into a car without suffering a strong physical reaction.

- An idealistic mission worker in an urban context suffers a mental and emotional breakdown following the murder of one of the women with whom she worked.

On Sunday morning, when congregations gather for worship, many come with soul wounds buried deep within from previous life experiences. Survivors of abuse, family members of those with addictions, and parents who have lost children are among those listening to sermons. Some soul wounds are rooted in a national event—those who have survived a mass shooting or those for whom the news coverage of the most recent national tragedy triggers memories of a violent experience in their own lives. Because these wounds are often hidden, preachers may not be aware of the dynamics at work.

Peter Levine describes those who suffer in this way: "They are unable to overcome the anxiety of their experience. They remain overwhelmed by the event, defeated and terrified. Virtually imprisoned by their fear, they are unable to re-engage in life. Others who experience similar events may have no enduring symptoms at all."[1]

Language about trauma and diagnosis of Posttraumatic Stress Disorder (PTSD) have become part of our national vernacular. Many may find the word *trauma* repelling or jarring and may be unaware of the importance of having precise language to name the complexities of how trauma affects individuals and groups. The word *trauma* is related to the ancient Greek word for "wound." The word *trauma* is important because it incorporates causal circumstances or events along with coping responses. Learning about trauma is beneficial for many because it helps them understand dynamics in their own lives or the lives of loved ones.

People who have experienced trauma of all kinds often share worldviews and behaviors caused by their experience of powerlessness, imminent death, and the ineffectiveness of language to help or describe their circumstances. Survivors of trauma struggle to feel safe, trust others, and find meaning in life. The past may be frozen in the moment in which the traumatic event occurred as the survivor experiences it again and again, unbidden, while the future is completely closed. The wound caused by trauma is deep—affecting the whole person. I use the term *soul wound* to speak of the pain that lingers within those who survive trauma and other wounding experiences.

Preachers today experience the pull of many possibilities and pressures. Sermons must contribute to congregational growth, encourage giving to support the church, avoid offending denominational leadership, teach the Bible, and speak a relevant and hopeful word for our time. This book doesn't seek to add one more burden to preachers but to shine the healing light of Christ on traumatic and other wounds carried by many in our world. The proposed methods and techniques may be helpful not only for survivors of trauma but also for others who feel the lingering effects of loss, bullying, or shame. The church has a unique and much needed balm for unhealed soul wounds. The Christian gospel travels through the cross to the resurrection, and the call to discipleship involves facing brokenness, pain, and loss armed with Christ's redemptive power.

To live fully into our calling, we who preach must do so with sensitivity and awareness toward those with soul wounds and a sense of hope and an

orientation toward God's promises of healing and new life. Every congregation includes people who carry soul wounds, leading to personal and social
ramifications for the individual and surrounding community. When pastors
encounter someone with a serious soul wound, listening and showing care
can be intuitive responses; so too may be the reflex to refer the person to a
professional counselor or mental health provider with more expertise in this
area. However, just because a referral has been made does not mean that the
congregation cannot be an agent of God's healing. Unsure of how to engage
wounded members in the midst of gathered church life, pastors may experience a sense of internal division between pastoral care that often happens in
private and the public ministries of preaching and worship. No matter how
uncomfortable or unqualified a pastor may feel when confronted by church
members with serious soul wounds, pastors cannot refer away their preaching ministry to everyone in the church.

Trauma-aware preaching can support healing for those with soul
wounds from trauma and other, less-raw painful memories. Sermons can
create a bridge between the gathered life of the congregation and care given
by the pastor or members of the congregation. Sermons can offer instruc-
tion about the pain of traumatic experience and legitimize the effects of
trauma. Sermons can reach out to those who may be suffering quietly and
provide an open door for further conversation. Preaching can speak God's
promises in a powerful way to those who need to hear them and provide
theological tools to help people make sense of their experiences in a way
that nurtures faith.

A starting place for speaking to those who have survived a traumatic experience can be marking the difference between healing and curing.[2] While
curing can be an instantaneous act of the Spirit in the present, curing most
often takes on eschatological dimensions, something that may not happen
this side of the realm of God. On the other hand, and from a Christian
perspective, healing is a process that is theologically rooted in the human
experiences of salvation and sanctification.[3] Healing can also be understood
as a fruit of the resurrection breaking into our world here and now. Healing can be personal, bodily, communal, relational, ecological, structural,
social, physical, or spiritual. When we see healing of any type in our world,
it is a sign of the resurrection regardless of whether it is claimed as such by
the ones who experience the healing. While PTSD is a complex illness and
trauma causes deep wounds, as Christians we believe that healing is part of
our experience of salvation. Healing is a process not to be confused with
curing. It is not some extra bonus gift that God capriciously doles out to
some believers and not others. Because we struggle with the eschatological

dimension of cures for the many wounds people carry, we may hesitate to talk about healing in our prayers and sermons. But we can ask God for healing with boldness. One of the ways that sin and brokenness affect us in our world is to blind us to signs of God's action among us. We can therefore also ask God to reveal healing that is already taking place so that we can name healing in our sermons.

What does it mean to be human in a world that stands between crucifixion and resurrection? In his essay "The Bitter Christ: Suffering and Spirituality in Denial," worship scholar Don Saliers addresses the necessity of dealing with complexity: "The mixed texture of our world—its terror and beauty—confronts our prayer and worship, our meditation and our liturgies. For increasing numbers of people the experience of the absence of God, or at least the loss of secure ideas of God, leads to giving up prayer and worship."[4] Trauma-informed pastors can preach sermons that are relevant for people with soul wounds from trauma and past life experiences and helpfully participate in the Spirit's work breaking cycles of violence and abuse. However, in order to participate in healing, preachers must be equipped to recognize what can cause soul wounds; to understand how these deep wounds may affect relationships, participation in church, and worship; and how to preach in ways that minister not only to survivors of trauma but also to the many who struggle to find healing and meaning for disappointment, loss, and other painful experiences and memories.

What Causes Soul Wounds?

People carry many types of wounds that may harm relationships and hinder their ability to experience love and hope. What causes these soul wounds? They are caused by experiences in which survivors feared for their own lives and well-being or that of others. Survivors often name a common set of experiences including feeling powerless in the face of danger, that language and other tools had little or no effect on their situation, and that structure or order in the world has been lost.

The *perception* of danger or threat may be more important than the *specific nature* of the experience. A person's background and prior experiences may make him or her more susceptible to complicating reactions in the wake of trauma. Just because someone has a traumatic experience does not mean that she or he will have a soul wound. However, as pastors and caregivers we may be watchful for signs of unhealed wounds. The following discussion may be helpful for pastors who seek to preach healing for a range of diverse wounds, those caused by unaddressed trauma as well as other more common painful experiences.

Not every traumatic event results in ongoing or lingering soul wounds. One clue that the event may be potentially wound-inducing is if someone describes her or his life with a clear sense of "before" and "after" surrounding a negative event. For example, more than twenty years ago a relative was involved in a serious car accident that left him paralyzed. This was an event with a clear "before" and "after" for his entire family, and for some time, they talked about life like this. Today, they no longer talk about life in this way. While he is still paralyzed, the traumatic wound around the accident has healed.

A serious car accident is only one example of a potentially trauma-inducing event. A wounding event can be "an intense one-time event, natural or human caused, where there is a serious threat of harm or death," such as a "natural disaster, accident, rape, or sudden loss."[5] Traumatic events can also involve ongoing situations or repeated events such as living in a violent context or having everyday encounters with racism or gender issues that chip away at dignity and safety over time.[6] These one-time events or repeated/ongoing situations can impact individuals as well as larger groups. Ongoing experiences of poverty or abuse can create traumatic wounds in addition to making an individual less resilient in the face of more common experiences of stress. Only the survivor can define an experience as traumatic, and not all traumatic experience leads to a lasting wound. Personality, history, and the presence or absence of a caring community can all affect experience of trauma.

Individuals can also experience secondary or vicarious trauma from hearing stories of those who have directly experienced trauma. This can happen in the case of first responders, family members and friends, lawyers or human-rights advocates, medical and mental health professionals, clergy, and those who operate crisis lines—anyone who "cares and listens to the stories of fear, pain, and suffering of others."[7] Secondary trauma can often have a cumulative impact over time that leads to "compassion fatigue." Yet the satisfaction that care-providers experience can help counteract the cumulative emotional wear-and-tear.[8]

Trauma can also be experienced by individuals who may have participated in causing pain to others, especially in cases where the harm was unintentional, such as in a car accident, as part of a medical procedure or drug trial gone wrong, or following orders in a military context.[9] This participation-induced trauma can also be called *moral injury*. Brite Divinity School's Soul Repair Center describes moral injury as growing from making decisions or witnessing actions that may violate moral values in the midst of life-or-death circumstances, often in a context of war or situation of violence and chaos following a mass shooting or terrorist attack. These decisions may cause a survivor to experience intense shame, loss, and disconnection from his or her core identity.[10]

Trauma can also be collective or societal, caused by one-time events or ongoing/repeated experiences. Examples of one-time events include large-scale natural disasters, such as the 2005 Indian Ocean Tsunami; human-induced disasters, such as a nuclear accident; deliberate actions from an enemy, such as a terrorist attack; political revolution that results in sudden cultural shifts, such as the Cultural Revolution in China; and the loss of a significant and symbolic leader, such as Gandhi or Martin Luther King Jr.[11] Repeated or cumulative experiences can include *historical trauma* with ongoing effects, such as slavery and racism in the United States or conflict between religious groups in the Middle East; *cultural trauma* in which a group experienced a complete or nearly complete destruction of culture, such as the case with Native Americans and Jewish people through the Shoah; and *structurally induced trauma* created by laws and cultural practices that result in injustice, such as Jim Crow laws or South African apartheid.[12] These events are complex and multifaceted. Collective or societal trauma can be traced to actions in multiple categories.[13] Hurricane Katrina would be an example of a multi-category catalyst for collective trauma, involving natural disaster as well as human error and racism.

Traumatic wounds can also be transferred from one generation to another through time as with the experience enslaved Africans brought to the United States, cultural and physical genocide of Native populations, and colonialism.[14] Because of the wide variability in reactions and triggering experiences, it is important for pastors to validate a traumatic reaction regardless of how the precipitating event or events may appear to others.[15] Many events and chronic conditions can cause trauma, from the murder of a colleague or car accident to childbirth, serious illnesses or pandemics, human-caused natural disasters such as an oil spill, homelessness, or being a refugee.[16] Because trauma impacts not only individuals but also groups, communities, and societies, we can see how wounds, both named and unnamed, are likely present in most ministry contexts.[17]

While serious trauma does not impact everyone in a congregation directly, it is beneficial for the life of the church for pastors to preach trauma-aware sermons. Some of the same symptoms and concerns faced by survivors of trauma are also challenges for people who have a wide range of painful experiences such as losing a job, bullying, or betrayal in relationship.

Encounters with pain and brokenness are part of life in a world still waiting for complete redemption. Further, while we pray otherwise, serious traumatic events may happen at any time. Trauma-aware preachers will be prepared to speak to the immediate situation and begin fostering healing. Even if not every member experiences trauma directly, when a brother or sister is hurting it affects the whole community. Like a human body, participants in a community are not completely independent of each other. Part of our identity as Christians is to care for the whole body in order to witness to Christ's healing intentions. When wounded members experience care and healing, the witness of the whole church is stronger.

Stress and Trauma

The effects of trauma are physical, emotional, cognitive, relational, sociological, and spiritual.[18] The field of trauma studies is like a fair or convention with various disciplines promoting their perspectives and wares. Expert insights range from clinical awareness brought by psychiatrists and neuroscientists to experiential knowledge from poets, memoirists, and anthropologists.[19] What these varied approaches confirm is the thoroughly penetrating impacts of trauma on survivors and their communities.

Soul wounds can arise from a range of causes and circumstances, but the physiological response to stress always simmers beneath the surface. According to the Strategies for Trauma Awareness and Resilience (STAR) program, "stress is any outside force or event that has an effect on the body, mind, or emotions. It is the automatic physical, mental, or emotional response to these events."[20] A stressful experience triggers neurochemicals and hormones in our bodies that stimulate us to act.[21] Not all stress is bad. At best, we can feel energized and motivated, such as the stress a student might feel in preparing for an exam, an athlete might feel before a big game, or a musician before a concert. At times we may feel unproductive stress, such as sitting in busy traffic as we watch the minutes tick by making us late for an appointment. These experiences of stress are fairly common and likely not wounding. However, prolonged stress can lead to fatigue, depression, and anxiety, which can make us more susceptible to deeper wounds that make it difficult to connect to others or experience God's presence and good news in our lives. Traumatic stress is different from other forms of stress in that it completely overwhelms a person so that his or her experience exceeds any ability to respond.[22]

Chapter 1

Responses to Traumatic Stress

It is important for us to realize that the reactions or coping mechanisms that emerge in the wake of a deep wounding experience are not usually a matter of choice but automatic physical, mental, emotional, and behavioral responses to ensure survival in the face of what feels like a deep threat. Like the sources of wounds themselves, responses and behaviors may vary depending on how long the wound has been present. Responses to traumatic stress are cross-culturally similar.[23]

The first series of responses are organized into a "survivor-victim cycle." Early responses include physiological changes, such as shutting down the cerebral cortex (or thinking brain) and operating primarily from the limbic system and amygdala that register fear, and the brain stem that has no sense of time other than an ongoing sense of "now" that controls instinctual actions.[24] This feels like a state of "hyper arousal," as heart rate and breathing increase, blood rushes to muscles, and senses are heightened. Less crucial body functions, such as digestion, shut down.[25] After the moment of danger, traumatized people may shake, cry uncontrollably, or sweat profusely.[26] Because these reactions may appear unseemly or embarrassing, most people will suppress them. Yet allowing the body to release traumatic energy can actually be beneficial for long-term healing.[27]

The physical responses to trauma have mental and cognitive dimensions that are important to understand. Dissociation, or a sense of detachment from what has happened, keeps people from being emotionally overwhelmed in the moment. Memories are not created or retained in the usual way and later produce extreme detail coupled with difficulty in recalling events.[28] Traumatic memories may return involuntarily with sensory details and a sense of collapsed time when the survivor encounters triggers, such as smell, sight, or sound.[29] When a traumatized person experiences an "intrusive memory" it is as if the event is happening again in real-time, and the body responds accordingly.[30] Fear of triggers and a sense that they should be "over it" can cause survivors to grow isolated as they withdraw from regular activities.[31] One of the impacts of unhealed traumatic wounds over time is that survivors operate using mainly lower-brain functions rather than the "thinking brain."[32] This means that survivors may not be capable of thinking through consequences, may speak or act without a filter, and may respond to relatively minor annoyances with extreme actions—akin to going after a mosquito with a gun.[33] When the frontal cortex re-engages, the person may feel ashamed or emotionally numb, or they may even deny what just happened.[34]

8

In addition to physical, mental, emotional, and relational responses, trauma also deeply affects a survivor's sense of self and spiritual grounding. Because trauma destroys meaning and harms a person's sense of identity and ability to make meaning from her or his life, a survivor may question God and may need access to different theology and different language to make sense of life.[35] Chronic or ongoing trauma can cause some physiological and emotional responses to become regular behavior. These adaptations can help people survive in dangerous settings, yet the effects can also be corrosive. Judith Herman observes that those who experience a single traumatic event may feel that they are "losing their minds" while those who experience chronic trauma feel that they have "lost themselves."[36] Wounding experiences also impact one's relationship with God. A survivor may wonder why God didn't intervene and struggle to make sense of what has happened.

Unhealed and unattended trauma does not just "go away." Rather, the pain is often transferred and the survivor may "get stuck" in a cycle of suffering and fear marked by a lack of power and hope.[37] PTSD is given as a diagnosis when severe responses to trauma persist for longer than one month.[38] Specific symptoms of PTSD often overlap with the immediate symptoms of trauma such as flashbacks to the event, symptoms of increased arousal such as inability to sleep, and finding patterns where none actually exist.[39] Some research shows that flashbacks are more than just "vivid memories" and are likely stored differently in the brain than typical memories.[40] Memories can usually be verbalized, but flashback memories exist beyond the scope of language, leading to frustration in explaining the experience to loved ones and professionals seeking to help.[41] Making sense of what happened and reconstructing a meaningful narrative account may be a helpful part of healing. When someone tells us that they suffer from PTSD, we know that they have survived a traumatic event. PTSD is the most widely recognized response to trauma in our broader cultural vernacular, but reducing all trauma to PTSD risks minimizing other responses to trauma that fall short of a specific diagnosis.[42]

Recognizing Unhealed Wounds

As ministers of the gospel with a calling to nuture faith and God's healing in the congregation, awareness of trauma is not only beneficial for pastoral care but for every part of ministry. Preaching is shaped by the context of the sermon and the situation of listeners. When that context includes unhealed wounds from trauma and other experiences, sermons can be shaped to bring God's healing and empowerment to these situations.

Survivors of trauma need spiritual care and support that may not be provided by those outside the church. This care may come in part through pastoral counseling, but preaching is also an important part of caring for indivuals as well as the whole community. Preaching with awareness of trauma legitimizes the experiences of survivors as well as others who have unhealed wounds from painful experiences and speaks God's love to those who need it. If preachers do not speak to these concerns, it implicitly communicates that the church—and, worse, that God—doesn't care. Nothing could be further from the truth.

Pastors and other caring friends may notice that someone who has come through trauma or another serious wounding experience may pull away from relationships, may be easily offended or hurt, may startle easily, and may experience physical symptoms that affect sleeping and eating. One who emerges from trauma may cognitively know the narrative around the wounding events but may not have corresponding personal memories. Instead she or he may have a series of images or sensations. These sensations may be triggers for flashbacks. For example, those who have experienced war may not enjoy celebrations with fireworks, as the noise is reminiscent of artillery bombardment. Some have described the experience of a flashback as similar to having a very vivid nightmare while being awake.[43]

The neurochemistry of a trigger is complex. The brain has the amazing capacity to grow new pathways as we move through life, which means that when a trigger becomes associated with a traumatic response, they can become "wired together" in the brain's neural pathways.[44] If we know that someone suffers traumatic responses from specific triggers, it can be helpful to ask what those triggers are. Awareness can help us create emotionally safe worship spaces.

Unfortunately, violence and trauma are often reciprocally related. A violent act or event may inflict a traumatic wound, and unaddressed and unhealed trauma can lead to more violence. Violent behavior may be mainly turned inward toward oneself through addictions, such as substance abuse, workaholism, eating disorders, or self-mutilation.[45] These behaviors are a form of distraction to keep the wounded person from being completely preoccupied with her or his wound. Despite attempts to distract themselves with other behaviors, "shame, dread, and helplessness are pervasive, alternating with numbness, depression, or a sense of emptiness. Their sense of agency is damaged; they often feel powerless and alone in a hostile world, wondering whether anyone cares if they live or die."[46] Spiritually, wounded people may wonder if God cares for them and how to find meaning in life amidst growing fear and disorientation.[47]

Some people with deep soul wounds turn their sense of violation outward in anger that drives toward a revenge-themed sense of justice.[48] They may fabricate a narrative around the theme of "good versus evil" making the "bad guy" seem less than human.[49] The stories victims tell can become repetitive so that an identity of victim-turned-avenger becomes formative, much like the origin story of the superhero Batman. While revenge fantasies may be normal in the wake of a wounding experience at the hands of a perpetrator, if these desires are unexamined and unchallenged the wounded person can become a violent wounder of others.[50] In the wake of mass shootings or home-grown terrorist attacks, stories often emerge that portray perpetrators as deeply wounded individuals. While these wounds do not justify violence, they serve as examples of some of the most extreme potential outcomes when people with unhealed soul wounds turn their inner pain outward toward others. James Gilligan, director of the Center for the Study of Violence at Harvard Medical School, observes, "All violence is an effort to do justice or undo injustice."[51]

Claiming Therapeutic Approaches for the Church

While a relatively small number of people in our congregations may carry wounds from major traumatic events, lower levels of pain and bitterness are widely present in our congregations. Associate clinical professor of psychology at Harvard Medical School Kaethe Weingarten's work is practical and broadly applicable to people with a wide range of wounding experiences. Her *Witnessing Project* hopes to raise awareness around the acts of violence we witness and cultivate ways to deal with the effects.[52] She uses the term "common shock" to emphasize that this experience is common, is part of simply being a person in our world, and isn't connected to mental health challenges that can accompany a diagnosis related to post traumatic responses.[53] The term "common" also connotes that we have these experiences in common with others. Weingarten holds that the difference for individuals between common shock and what becomes an ongoing traumatic wound may have more to do with a community's response, presence, and action or lack of action than with the nature of the event.[54] Weingarten's work not only seeks to encourage healing and humanizing responses but to change "toxic witnessing" into "compassionate witnessing with others."[55] The concept of common shock expands the sense of who needs healing words. People in our congregations may experience a traumatic reaction even if they experience an event indirectly.

Compassionate Witness

The potential for common shock has only increased in recent years. Cameras are ever-present and videos of distressing events are readily posted or broadcast live on social media platforms. People can watch immediately on phones whether commuting to work on the train, waiting in line, at work, or at school. Every day children and adults witness numerous violent or wounding actions that may range from seeing an animal hit by a car, hearing a news story about assault, watching the count of dead bodies rise after a natural disaster half-way around the world, or seeing a video of police shooting a suspect. When we are exposed to violent actions in the news or elsewhere, we can experience different responses. Some may move into denial, setting up a psychological wall or barrier to keep it away. Some may strive to be strong and unmoved in the face of violence in our world, particularly violence that feels distant from us. When violence feels nearer to us or to those we love, we can become numb or emotionally and spiritually eroded and susceptible to physiological traumatic response.

In the face of such challenges, Weingarten advocates for another approach. She defines "compassionate witness" as that which "helps us recognize our shared humanity, restore our sense of common humanity when it falters, and block our dehumanizing others."[56] Witnesses of a wide range of varied acts of violence and micro aggressions may feel tempted to "checkout" or look the other way. The challenge for compassionate witnesses is to "stay present."[57] Compassionate witnessing is implicit in many group contexts such as AA or NA where listeners serve a role as witness to another's truth-telling and offer accountability in a journey toward healing that at times involves coming to terms with traumatic events done to or by the one who is sharing with the group. Staying present and attentive to listeners is particularly crucial for preaching as it encourages shared vulnerability and sharing the compassionate presence of Christ, particularly in any congregational response that may follow the sermon.

Christians can find theological roots for compassionate witnessing in the very heart of God. In the Old Testament, God is described as compassionate. Exodus, Deuteronomy, Psalms, Lamentations, and Isaiah all name God's compassion.[58] A Hebrew word for compassion, *rachamim,* has a deeply visceral connotation.[59] Theologian Andrew Purves links the Hebrew sense of compassion to the word *rechem,* which means womb. The "literal" meaning of compassion is "the womb pained in solidarity with the suffering of another."[60] "God's womb" aches when God's people suffer. Unpacking this biblical language for compassion helps us to see God's compassion as deeply generative and creative, which sets a stage for our own compassion to not be an end in itself or just emotional but bodily and generative too.[61]

Weingarten outlines three steps for compassionate witnessing with great potential for preaching and worship: (1) choosing a reasonable and manageable focus for witness; (2) carefully and compassionately listening and responding; and (3) engaging in a literal or symbolic action that addresses the need of the other.[62] Pastors can help congregations define a manageable focus in the way they shape a narrative of troubling events in the sermon. Preachers contribute to a compassionate response by listening and with permission giving voice to traumatic experience. Sermons can also suggest symbolic action, which could take place in the context of worship in addition to offering testimony concerning the entire compassionate witnessing event. For example, the crash of a bus carrying the junior hockey team of the town of Humboldt, Saskatchewan, killing sixteen and injuring many more, caused lasting trauma for that town and common shock for many. Hockey players and fans from around the world responded with acts of compassionate witness. Many placed hockey sticks outside their homes in remembrance of the dead and injured and people across Canada wore hockey jerseys several days after the accident.[63] The mayor of Toronto declared April 12, "Jersey Day."[64] While this example represents a response from broader culture, the same process holds rich potential for the church to respond to the myriad of common everyday shocks and losses that we experience. Congregations can engage in communal acts of compassionate witness during worship and preachers can suggest actions, frame already existing practices, or share stories of actions in sermons. Benefits of this approach are that it is attainable rather than overwhelming and it keeps witnesses from feelings of helplessness and despair.

The church has tremendous potential for compassionate witness and for supporting other witnesses. However, this is only possible when our compassion is grounded in Jesus Christ and preachers are vulnerable, humble, and present to the Spirit's stirring in the preaching moment. Preachers can use stories of compassionate witness in their sermons as examples of faith in action, but also of God in action. Preaching to others in the midst of despair and brokenness is a privilege, impossible to undertake apart from the power of Christ. Pastoral theologian Deborah Hunsinger puts it well,

God alone can bear the sins of the world and not be destroyed by them. God alone can witness the horror and terror of what human beings are capable of inflicting on one another. In Jesus Christ, God takes the suffering of the world into his own capacious heart and ministers openly or secretly, through the power of the Holy Spirit to every creature in distress.[65]

Reasonable Hope

Part of the process of healing is acknowledging that healing may co-exist alongside brokenness and despair. Healing does not always involve curing. Besides offering practices that foster compassionate witnessing in the midst of common shock experiences, Kaethe Weingarten also developed the practice of "reasonable hope."[66] Reasonable hope is a community sustained practice rather than an individual feeling.[67] Reasonable hope engages with the here and now rather than a distant eschatological event. She encourages practitioners to live hope as a verb rather than as a noun because focusing on the action invokes and empowers God and us as subjects, rather than as passive recipients of either "having" hope or "not having" hope.[68] Reasonable hope operates under the assumption that the future is open and has not been decided; this belief is expressed through prayer.[69] Yet reasonable hope also offers a somewhat "limited horizon of expectations" that can help people move from situations of deep pain, suffering, and hopelessness toward a life that is better.[70]

Weingarten's practical view of hope arises from her concern that people become overwhelmed by brokenness. By engaging with practices around reasonable hope, "even while one cannot do everything one can do something, goals and pathways into the future are formed."[71] Weingarten calls reasonable hope, "humble hope."[72] It operates under the same principles that remind us that "perfect" is the enemy of "good." In Weingarten's words, "It allows reasonable goals to trump ideal ones. It is satisfied to do less than everything that needs to be done in order to ensure that something be done."[73] She writes, "Small actions need not be trivial. They may have ripple effects."[74]

Practicing reasonable hope means engaging with concrete principles. Among them are these three: (1) Reasonable hope involves action or a set of actions that move a person toward a goal more than a feeling; (2) reasonable hope can and often does exist alongside doubt and even despair; and (3) other people can help someone with reasonable hope, both in envisioning and in the concrete steps needed to move toward a goal.[75]

One of the most insidious symptoms of unhealed soul wounds is that they rob people of hope. When those we love lose hope, we can engage practices of reasonable hope to offer incremental steps toward a future. Sometimes these incremental steps can be shockingly simple and tangible. Weingarten's daughter, Miranda, has a serious disability. Shortly before a concert that Miranda was looking forward to participating in, she had an insensitive and cruel medical appointment. Weingarten asked her daughter what she could offer to sustain her in the moment and get to the concert. Her daughter responded, "white chocolate."[76]

Weingarten outlines a set of supportive practices for those in the midst of pain from wounding experiences.[77] They may also be helpful for those who accompany wounded people on a journey to healing: "Listening without my own agenda; opening myself to sorrow; finding connection in loss; attending to the present; resting within uncertainties; accepting fear; tending my relationship to aloneness; believing that there is always something that can be sustaining; working for a preferred identity; and relating intimately and collaboratively."[78] Preachers can be on the lookout for these behaviors in our world. Sermons can name and nurture them as gifts of the Spirit and fractional glimpses of our ultimate hope in Jesus Christ who completely opened himself to these same experiences and overcame death so that pain, fear, and loss might not have the final say in our lives and future.

In the resurrection of Jesus Christ we have access to an "unreasonable" hope; a hope that is beyond the realm of what is normally possible. As preachers and Christian leaders, we are the keepers and proclaimers of this hope and we name it again and again. We join a chorus of other witnesses across time and proclaim this unreasonable hope even when people suffer and stagger under the weight of wounding experiences.

It is common, normal, and natural for those who are in the midst of suffering and trauma to waiver in belief. On July 4, 2016, my sister-in-law Twila died from a brain aneurysm. She was a healthy mother in her thirties with young children who had no prior symptoms. Following Twila's death, my father-in-law struggled with the promises of God.[79] He couldn't stand to hear the promise in Romans 8:38 that "nothing separates us from God's love." He felt distant from God's love.

In the midst of trauma, loss, and soul wounds, focusing on a reasonable hope may be a helpful intermediary point and appropriate tool when theologically framed as a fragmentary glimpse of God's fuller promises of new life. Part of the calling for preachers is to bear witness to and thereby amplify the small steps and moments of progress, pointing out God's divine signature in the lower corner of the sermonic portraits we paint.[80] We also strive to proclaim hope that listeners in our congregations can hear and receive in challenging and painful times. "Reasonable hope coexists with doubt and despair." It is hope for all of us who are caught in the messy eschatological realities of a world that still suffers, but where we are also graced with the presence of the living Christ and glimpses of God's realm breaking in among us.[81]

Weingarten's research shows that encounters with hope over time can build resilience in people before they experience trauma.[82] People who grow in resilience are able to experience more hope.[83] Preaching that explicitly shares stories of hope serves as a kind of inoculation that can help prevent soul wounds before they start—or at least lessen their impact. Similarly, for us as preachers, the act of looking specifically for signs of God at work in our world changes us and makes us more resilient to traumatic experiences, whether in our own lives or in the lives of those we accompany in ministry. When people cannot get to hope on their own, Weingarten insists that vicarious hope can help.[84] We can "do" hope for others in our sermons, build resilience, and contribute to God's actions of healing.

Weingarten's writing is peppered with stories of hope that serve as smaller practical signs of God's incremental healing. She talks about a man who expanded his self-understanding by looking at his childhood from another angle, which gave him tools to build stronger relationships, and a woman who found that she could set boundaries around her relationship with her young adult daughter. By saying no to the daughter who phoned to vent her anxieties, the woman was less drained and able to extend love. Another woman volunteers with former girl soldiers, now mothers, who gave birth while fighting alongside rebel groups in Uganda. She sees signs of joy amidst the suffering and rejection that these women experience as they support one another and break into spontaneous songs together in their camp.[85] These stories are not perfect and don't involve tidy and complete fairy-tale endings but they are hopeful and represent practical steps toward our gospel hope rooted in the coming realm of God.

Weingarten notes that people often experience hope when barriers to love are torn down.[86] If we are experiencing an upsurge in despair or loss in the wake of a wounding experience, we may want to focus our gaze on where we can find love and make the path between us and love as direct as possible. Weingarten notes that therapists must love their clients.[87] The same is true for pastors. We must love our congregations and preach in a way that enacts that love. As preachers we can clearly proclaim the unbounded love of God directed toward people in our sermons while also showing how God removes barriers between people in our world. If we find ourselves feeling hopeless in ministry, it can help to look for where love is being blocked in our own lives.

Contextual Awareness and Flexibility

Traumatic experiences are part of the context of our preaching, regardless of the background or location of our congregations. Twenty-five percent of the global population lives in the midst of high levels of criminal violence.[88] Ten percent of all girls experience forced sexual acts.[89] Thirty-five percent of all women and ten percent of men experience intimate partner violence.[90] Our nation is grappling with opioid abuse and mass incarceration.[91] Unless they share their pain with us as pastors, we may not know what private wounds are aching in people's souls as they come to worship. Hunsinger poignantly wonders, "Is it possible to talk about trauma without causing pain to those already bearing trauma in their bodies and souls? Daily through the media, we are bombarded with stories capable of breaking our hearts, yet little attention is given to the impact of such accounts on their hearers. How do we bear these stories with an open heart? Indeed, how do we bear them at all?"[92] The pulpit does not need to become a trauma center to deal with the realities of stress and trauma in congregations. Preachers nonetheless need to be aware how they can speak to trauma without raising it each week.

When a large-scale tragedy strikes, preachers have an opportunity to nurture healing before wounds have a chance to deepen. On a Friday afternoon in the midst of Advent 2012, a desperate and mentally ill young man took the life of his mother, twenty first-graders, and six teachers and staff from the Sandy Hook elementary school in Newtown, Connecticut. The horrific and heart-breaking news dominated the media that weekend as pastors and church leaders prepared for Sunday morning worship. Our church had planned a special seasonal service focused on music with a children's choir and other ensembles. The groups had been planning for weeks and leaders decided to carry on with worship as usual. The worship leader did acknowledge the tragedy at Newtown in her welcoming comments and opening prayer, but otherwise the service went on as planned, albeit with a muted tone rather than a raucously joyful one. By moving forward with business as usual, the congregation missed an opportunity to acknowledge and validate church members' experiences of this gun-inflicted wound in the soul of our nation. The preacher missed a chance to speak a word of Advent hope in the midst of devastation.

For those who have experienced prior trauma, these events may trigger a return to the previous wounding experience or a spiral into depression or hopelessness. Positively, it is never too late for God to bring healing to a wound. A triggering event in the present may provide an opportunity for new awareness of the painful effects of the wound and God's power to heal.

Some congregations are able to be flexible in the wake of traumatic experience, much like a palm tree bends in hurricane-force winds. When my sister-in-law died, it was not only a tragedy for our family. Twila was very involved in her local church and its various programs. She was a leader on church committees and ran the projection system for the congregation during worship. News of her death was so shocking for the community that the pastors decided to shift their worship plans to reflect on "God's covenant in times of trouble," a continuation of a series on covenant, rather than moving on to a new worship series as originally planned. They did not seek to make the service another funeral, but an opportunity for the community to respond to Twila's death together with quiet, listening, sharing, and lament in the presence of God. This is not the first time this congregation has changed plans to respond to a tragedy in the community. They engaged in a similar service following the sudden death of a toddler in the congregation. By being willing to bend, adapt, and engage with painful experiences of brokenness, this congregation implicitly witnesses to God's stake in these events. God and God's people care about our pain and loss.

Attending to Whole Persons

By participating in healing from soul wounds we are attending to people as whole persons. The church has long tended to focus on right beliefs, separating spirituality from the physical body. Interestingly, this sense of separating soul from body is often described by survivors of traumatic events and can be part of the "freeze" response.[93] The person becomes detached from the present. Many speak of being unable to move physically, even to defend themselves. "Victims of sexual assault, for instance, sometimes speak of 'leaving their body' and watching themselves from another point in the room: standing next to the bed or looking down from the ceiling."[94] Many who suffer the worst effects of unhealed soul wounds have little awareness of what is happening in their bodies. Studies show that this approach can actually make people more susceptible to traumatic wounds as well as to harmful conditions such as heart attacks, strokes, and physical collapse.[95]

While we may find ourselves operating according to the "myth" that those who have a strong faith should be able to remain relaxed or calm with few or no adverse physical reactions or feelings, the truth is that "it is virtually impossible to remove all of the physiological reactions to stress and trauma."[96] By openly acknowledging wounding experiences and lingering wounds in sermons we de-stigmatize human responses to these and other less severe experiences of brokenness and pain in our world. We can begin to help listeners to be more aware of what is happening in their own bodies, which can open them to deeper experiences of healing and build resilience against future traumatic experiences.

Healing from traumatic wounds involves facing what happened and going down into the accompanying fear in the presence of another.[97] It can involve reconstructing a narrative of events. It can involve making sense of, or finding a way to ascribe meaning to, what happened. Counterintuitively, talking about or trying to directly process the traumatic or wounding event can cause harm. Pastors need to tread lightly and let the wounded person take the lead. A preaching class provides an opportunity for unusually direct feedback. In one of our student preaching sessions, a particularly vivid and troubling story elicited responses from classmates who had survived traumatic experiences saying that on a "bad day" such a description may have triggered a flashback or another harmful response. Deborah Hunsinger compassionately writes, "Trauma survivors need to choose life over death, not once but many times, reaching out with the fragile hope that the trauma can be healed or transformed, that the pain will abate, or that some kind of normalcy will return."[98]

Theological Frameworks for Addressing Unhealed Wounds

We have already laid some groundwork for understanding healing as a gift of salvation that can be experienced by all and noted the eschatological dimensions around the slow process of healing as we encounter fragmentary glimpses of God's realm breaking into our world. Healing comes to us as a foretaste of God's intentions for all of creation.

In the midst of the pain of unhealed trauma, the church has theological frameworks that support approaches to preaching as a means of participating in God's healing of traumatic wounds. Part of the challenge of practical theology in the midst of trauma is navigating the tension between claiming our ultimate hope in Jesus Christ and being pastorally and contextually sensitive preachers amidst horrific realities that mark life this side of the realm of God. Our faith may call us to absolute proclamation of life in the face of death, but we may also wonder what good our words are if listeners shut down. We need to embrace both, proclaiming a word of life in ways that can bring comfort and peace to hurting lives. To this end, I will explore two theological perspectives with potential to move survivors toward healing.

Understanding the Dynamic of Han

Theologian Andrew Park moves beyond traditional theological understandings of personal direct agency and human sin. *Han* is an anguished wound created in those who are oppressed or sinned against, particularly recurrently.[99] *Han* is the unhealed wound carried by survivors of traumatic experience. Park uses evocative terms to describe the wound: "boxed-in hope," "collapsed feeling of anguish," "unfathomable wound," "emotional heart attack," "void of abysmal grief."[100] Park recognizes that descriptive words cannot do justice to the concept of *han,* and so recounts stories of those who have survived horrific exploitation, such as Jewish people who survived Nazi concentration camps and victims of abuse and incest.[101]

Han can be individual, collective, conscious, and unconscious, with both active and passive signs. In situations of conscious *han* where there is a clear person or object that was the source of the traumatic suffering, active responses include all-consuming revenge.[102] This violence can also be enacted inwardly through forms of self-harm and self-hatred when a specific offender can't be named or is too powerful to confront.[103] *Han* that bubbles beneath consciousness can emerge as a posture of "bitterness" in the active form and "helplessness" in the passive form.[104] Naomi in the biblical story of Ruth is an example of *han* manifesting in bitterness after watching her husband and sons die far from home. Because she is concerned for her survival, there is no time to reflect. She expresses the bitterness of *han* as she and Ruth struggle to survive.[105] In her *han* she is unrecognizable to herself and asks for others to call her "Mara," a name that means "bitter." Ultimately Naomi finds healing and transformation through God's empowerment and raising up of a protector and heir. Less active unconscious *han* can be expressed through passive helplessness.[106] Collectively, active forms of *han* can lead to revolution and the creation of racist or bias-based behaviors and systems, more passive forms find expression in despair and creation of spirituals and other laments.[107]

Sin unfolds relationally so that *han* is a by-product of sin and also creates more sin in a cyclical pattern. The one who has been wounded often becomes a wounder of others.[108] God attends to the different needs of wounder and wounded to stop the cycle. The wounder suffers from guilt, while the wounded person experiences shame.[109] Guilt and shame are associated with transgressed boundaries. The one who has been violated experiences shame for not having been able to stop the violation from occurring.[110] Shame is associated with lack of self-esteem and being disempowered. Park names different types of shame, which may be experienced by those who have survived a wounding experience, including humiliation, failure, disgrace, and collective humiliation.[111] For example, a survivor of rape not only experiences the initial physical violation but also endures humiliating medical examination, a trial, and media scrutiny.[112] Park writes, "The shame that the victim experiences devastates her human dignity and inner space, haunting all aspects of her life."[113] Guilt is experienced by those who cause harm to others—this can also be trauma inducing. Appropriate guilt can lead to reparations and repaired social relationships.[114] Both shame and guilt can lead to anger. For survivors, anger can be helpfully channeled into individual and communal restorative acts of resistance.[115]

Like traditional theology, our church processes have tended to focus more on the sin of perpetrators rather than the wounds of those who have been sinned against. This mirrors how criminal justice systems work in the West; however, Park notes that it does not reflect God's sense of justice. While God hears and receives the prayers of both parties—the sinner who seeks forgiveness and the sinned against who seeks justice and healing, God is not impartial. God stands with the sinned-against who bear the wound of *han*.[116]

Because the criminal justice system and many other systems—such as those in schools and even church institutions—tend to focus on perpetrators rather than victims, there is space for congregations to step in and address those who have been ignored. Survivors of trauma need to experience liberation as much as perpetrators need to experience repentance and forgiveness. Understanding *han* gives preachers a greater vocabulary in understanding the dynamics of sin and brokenness. Preaching about trouble we experience will resonate with wounded listeners when it doesn't only focus on things that we have done wrong but also addresses wrongs that have been done to us—either directly or indirectly. God offers especially devoted love for those who have been on the receiving end of sin and brokenness. Jesus's woundedness brings *han* into the life of God and God transforms woundedness into healing.[117] By offering God's love to wounded victims, we can participate in God's promise of peace by interrupting cycles that can lead to violence toward others or toward the self.

Theology of Remaining

Shelly Rambo's theological work around trauma seeks to name and claim a middle territory, the space of "Holy Saturday," the space between Good Friday and Easter Sunday. Her work draws from the pattern many experience in processing traumatic experience, which often involves the initial traumatic experience, intense fear of the event recurring, and sometimes re-experiencing the event through flashbacks. The wound of trauma is created and deepened by the unfinished experience, the sense that the traumatic experience is still unfolding.[118]

Rambo seeks to develop this "middle" space between the cross and resurrection as a place of connection and healing for trauma survivors where the good news is not either the cross or resurrection but the movement between these events. Jesus's experience of death on a cross is not the end of his journey; he moves from cross through the middle ground to resurrection life.[119] Standing with those who are suffering in the "middle" keeps us from glossing over traumatic experience in a rush to get to the resurrection.[120] As Rambo puts it, "Without witnessing to what does not go away, to what remains, theology fails to provide a sufficient account of redemption."[121]

For preachers, this means resisting the urge to preach "tidy" grace, avoiding easy answers and symmetrical stories where the exact trouble introduced earlier in the sermon is completely resolved, sermons where the puppy is lost in the introduction and found again in the conclusion, where every illness is cured, where every broken marriage is saved. While we should never deny God's miraculous action, we would do well to explore whether the good news we preach will ring true from the vantage point of life in the middle. From the middle, a story of a judge sentencing a drug addict to a jail term can be grace in that it saves the addict's life. From the middle, a story about caring hospice workers who love and attend to dying patients can be a sign of God's presence and action in our world.

Unaddressed and unhealed soul wounds can color an entire community's witness. Our world is changed by traumatic violence and we all experience the ramifications. Rambo asserts that engaging with the middle is not only necessary for attending to those with traumatic wounds, but is important for all of us.[122] Our lives are bound together so that, for example, my sister's wound is also painful to me. Rambo seeks power in testimony as we seek to bring voice to that which defies language.[123] The power of God, the love of God, and the pain of human violence all stretch the limits of what we can express in language and metaphor. Yet, this too is the calling of preaching and God equips us for the task at hand as we carefully attend to the language we use and the purposes behind that language.[124]

Positively, Rambo sees the lens of traumatic experience as a gift rather than a problem that we must solve. She writes, "The insights of trauma actually constitute the hermeneutical lens through which an alternative theological vision of healing and redemption emerges. This lens casts the relationship between death and life in the Christian narrative in a much more complex light. Trauma is the key to articulating a theology of redemption rather than the problem around which theology must navigate."[125] She likens trauma to a "shattered lens" that impacts how the world is seen but through which we can also see new things.[126]

As pastors and Christians, we inhabit an eschatological middle space between the advents of Christ empowered by the Spirit of God who stays with us. This same Spirit comforts survivors of trauma. This Spirit-breath exhaled by Jesus on the cross remains lovingly present with creation before the resurrection and enters Jesus's disciples who testify to the persistent "primal breath of God."[127] In the wake of trauma, language evades and survivors may struggle to find structure and meaning. In the middle, the Spirit "directs" and "gives form to the chaos."[128]

Not only are the cross and resurrection events that occur out of time, impacting creation before and after Jesus's death and resurrection, but so too is Holy Saturday, which is the space between. While still pre-resurrection, the middle is a Spirit-infused space of "second beginnings," where "the Spirit searches for forms of life where life cannot be easily recognized as such."[129] Further, the Spirit is not relegated to a linear form of time. Rather than reading the narrative from death to resurrection in a linear way, Rambo follows Hans Urs Von Balthazar in finding meaning in the timeless abyss of Holy Saturday.[130] "In the 'second chaos,' the recreation, the Spirit oscillates, turning not simply forward but back and forth."[131]

This sense of being outside of linear time relates to those who have experienced trauma. Past traumatic events may invade the present and present life may pale in comparison to vivid memories or flashbacks. Further, the experience of tragedy changes our relationship with time. Rambo writes, "Tragedies have no clear beginnings or endings; instead, they narrate events as if they are part of an endless cycle of existence."[132] Our experiences of grief are often cyclical. We experience grief afresh when a loved one who has died is not present for significant events. We may miss a lost job or a former home around particular seasons in the year, for example, a former teacher may feel loss when September rolls around. Following my sister-in-law Twila's death, our niece's first day of junior kindergarten was painful because we knew that Twila would have been so proud of her daughter. These experiences show us that our experiences in time may not always be linear. These cycles are often more pronounced for those who have experienced trauma.

Even for preachers who proclaim the resurrection of Christ, celebration of Holy Saturday is a significant reminder that victory does not always come immediately.[133] The hope of the middle, between life and death, is that God's breath persists and remains with us in love.[134] Rambo focuses on the Spirit that remains, but in our theological traditions, Jesus is still doing redemptive work on Holy Saturday. He descends into hell and releases those imprisoned there. For trauma survivors living through hell-on-earth, this is a powerful promise that we can name in preaching. In sermons we can appropriate Rambo's work on the "middle" by not leaping from trouble to a perfect or easy gospel. Showing how grace is often incremental may ring true to those with wounds from traumatic experience.

Conclusions: Moving toward Healing

Every congregation is touched by trauma. We have already noted the theological tension between our Christian hope and the challenges of preaching to wounded people. The horror of trauma is well documented and must never be minimized. Engaging with those who have experienced trauma is not for the faint of heart and preachers and other caregivers should not enter into relationships with naivete or optimism built on well-meaning platitudes. PTSD is a serious diagnosis and those who have experienced trauma or who have symptoms of PTSD should be under the care of professionals who are trained and experienced in dealing specifically with trauma. However, as Christians who believe in the God who brings new life from death, the horror of trauma is not the final verdict and preachers can play an important role in fostering avenues for God's healing, not only for serious trauma for but a wide range of experiences of brokenness, despair, and loss.

The next chapter turns to the Bible as a resource for preaching healing for those with soul wounds. I will offer five interpretive tools for preachers and demonstrate how these tools can be part of a trauma-informed process of moving from biblical text to sermon creation.

Chapter 2
Soul Wounds in the Bible

The Bible is a powerful tool for preachers seeking to bring trauma awareness and healing into sermons. Signs of trauma and resilience are found throughout scripture. For example, numerous biblical women suffer from infertility. Families experience the sudden death of loved ones, and people experience loss of home, community, and familiar patterns of life. Much of the Old Testament was written and edited by survivors of trauma associated with the Babylonian exile, and the earliest New Testament scriptures also address a traumatized community in the wake of Jesus's crucifixion and the persecution of his followers.

Perhaps the most powerful takeaway from a survey of scripture through the lens of trauma is that God's people survived these experiences not as shattered or hollow victims but as powerful witnesses and instruments for God in the world.[1] The resilience of God's people is amazing. Again and again God chooses to use those who have been wounded. With healing comes the promise that loss and brokenness are not the final verdict on one's sense of usefulness and purpose in the world. It is also possible that, as Paul said, God can work all things together for good (Rom 8:28); some people who survive trauma can experience a sense of freedom and become less entrenched in the existing order. Those who have experienced healing in the face of trauma are often less afraid of something completely new. Their witness can be a powerful gift for our churches today and can help all of us envision and imagine the realm of God even in places that look broken and forlorn.

Of course, the Bible is far more than these recorded experiences; it is God's Word. It serves as means of holy access to our God who accompanies and sustains in the midst of trauma, takes on suffering on our behalf, heals, and transforms us into the likeness of Christ.

The first part of this chapter will look at the Bible through the lenses of trauma and resilience aided by five interpretive tools that can be applied to scripture and our world. The second part of the chapter demonstrates these tools as part of a trauma-aware process for preachers to move from the biblical text to sermon creation by working through Genesis 22. Interpretive sensitivity and a trauma-aware approach to the Bible provide a firm foundation for healing proclamation.

Interpretive Tools

The Bible is a powerful resource for preaching to any human experience, not least wounded listeners. The following interpretive tools emerge from reading the Bible with awareness of trauma and can be used in preaching to create healing connections between the experiences of those with soul wounds and scripture.

1. Scripture as a Source of the Language of Faith

The Russian poet Anna Akhmatova's poem "Requiem" opens with a window into the traumatic experience of women standing in line outside a prison where their loved ones are suffering. Someone in the line recognizes the poet and asks in a whisper, "Can you describe this?" She responds, "I can!"[2] Many survivors of trauma struggle to find language to talk about their experiences. Biblical poets and authors have described numerous wounding and traumatic experiences. Preachers can harness these words to bring voice to the pain survivors experience in a safe way that is somewhat removed from the actual traumatic event and steeped in the Christian tradition of biblical language as the language of faith in worship, proclamation, and prayer.

In the face of soul-wounding trauma, the Babylonian exiles processed their experiences through description and poetry. We can trace Judah's expression of soul wounds in the book of Lamentations and in the Psalter. Lamentations describes the destruction of Jerusalem and the Temple, an event many had thought impossible.[3] Lamentations gives voice to the city itself personified as a grieving woman.[4] Lamentations frequently turns to self-blame to explain the catastrophic destruction of Jerusalem and calls upon God to hear Judah's prayer for restoration. Lamentations is one of the few biblical books to end with an uncertain or questioning tone.

Why do you forget us continually;
    why do you abandon us for such a long time?
Return us, Lord, to yourself. Please let us return!
    Give us new days, like those long ago—
unless you have completely rejected us,
    or have become too angry with us.[5]

Psalm 137 speaks evocatively and directly about the pain of exile.

Alongside Babylon's streams, there we sat down,
    crying because we remembered Zion.
We hung our lyres up in the trees there
    because that's where our captors asked us to sing;
our tormentors requested songs of joy:
    "Sing us a song about Zion!" they said.
But how could we possibly sing the Lord's song on foreign soil?

Jerusalem! If I forget you,
    let my strong hand wither!
Let my tongue stick to the roof of my mouth if I don't remember you,
    if I don't make Jerusalem my greatest joy.[6]

Painful memories expressed in Psalm 137 may have helped bind exiles together across geographic and generational distance.[7] Life expectancy was short enough that within the fifty years of exile, the generation who remembered Jerusalem would have mostly passed away.[8]

Preachers can also use biblical language to externalize the pain of wounding experiences today. Israelite exiles model this practice in their redaction and appropriation of Jeremiah's prophetic words. Jeremiah's calling to preach an unpopular prophetic word caused him to be hated and isolated from his peers.[9] Jeremiah's suffering was palpable and vivid. His words found resonance with his people, whose suffering in exile mirrored his own.[10] In David Carr's words, adding to and focusing on Jeremiah's words provided a means for exiles to "dissociate from their own pain, to speak of it in third person."[11] This provided an opportunity to externalize their experience as a safe way to process their trauma before integrating the experience into a new self-identity. This act of externalizing can be seen in those with severe soul wounds today. It can bring people out of paralyzing isolation and help them process and engage with their experiences in a way that doesn't re-traumatize.[12]

Preachers can assist in this practice by blending our discussion of the biblical text and our world in such a way that we put biblical language in the mouths of present-day figures. For example, using Jeremiah, preachers may allow the prophet's words to be our words as we suffer: "I can't stand the pain! My heart pounds, as I twist and turn in agony."[13] Similarly, God's promises to Jeremiah in his calling can be extended to us, "My power will make you strong like a fortress or a column of iron or a wall of bronze."[14]

2. Assigning Blame

A significant part of the journey to healing traumatic wounds is trying to make sense of what happened. Often this involves finding a cause, someone or something to blame. Pastors may struggle when they encounter this impulse in survivors of trauma, but preaching can sound hollow to listeners with wounded souls when it denies this very common and instinctual human drive. Highlighting this same practice in the Bible allows preachers to lift it up as a normal response in making an application to the experience of survivors today.

In the Old Testament, those who experience deeply wounding traumatic experiences tend to blame themselves or God. Both responses are normal and can be stages in moving toward healing. Because they unfold in a nexus of God's relationship with people, wounding experiences recorded in scripture explicitly invite God to be an active partner in processing these wounds. Even biblical figures blaming God and some of the negative or violent images surrounding God's agency in suffering found in the Old Testament can be viewed as "life-giving rhetoric" in that it keeps relationship with God alive in the midst of horrific circumstances.[15]

Blaming God

Some psalms call God to account for not holding to promises made toward David and David's line. Psalm 89 starts by recalling God's gracious acts on behalf of Israel but moves toward calling God to keep God's word to David,

> You've canceled the covenant with your servant.
> You've thrown his crown in the dirt.
> You've broken through all his walls.
> You've made his strongholds a pile of ruins.

All those who pass by plunder him.
　　He's nothing but a joke to his neighbors.
You lifted high his foes' strong hand.
　　You gave all his enemies reason to celebrate.
Yes, you dulled the edge of his sword
　　and didn't support him in battle.
You've put an end to his splendor.
　　You've thrown his throne to the ground.
You've shortened the prime of his life.
　　You've wrapped him up in shame.

How long will it last, LORD?
　　Will you hide yourself forever?
　　How long will your wrath burn like fire?
Remember how short my life is!
　　Have you created humans for no good reason?
Who lives their life without seeing death?
　　Who is ever rescued from the grip of the grave?
Where now are your loving acts from long ago, my Lord—
　　the same ones you promised to David by your own faithfulness?[16]

The move to blame God when terrible things happen has a long scriptural tradition. While Judah's unfaithfulness may be partly at root, blame too rests with God if God does not act to restore David's line. Blaming God does not signal a lack of faith. While it may make us uncomfortable, we must trust that God is big enough to handle these anguished cries. It is not the preacher's job to defend God. Blaming God for not acting signals a strong belief in the power of God and trust that God will act to bring justice, although it is not in our power to force God's hand. Preachers who cry out to God to be faithful to God's promises stand in a long scriptural tradition.

Self Blame

Amidst the horrors of Assyria's invasion and the complete destruction of the northern kingdom of Israel, the prophet Hosea offered a traumatized community a way to make meaning of their situation.[17] Prevailing religious thought at the time held that worshiping and making sacrifice to as many gods as possible would ensure greater safety and prosperity. However, Hosea's proclamation named Israel's promiscuous worship as akin to adultery in a relationship with Yahweh, whose covenantal relationship with Israel was in part defined by being their only God.[18] Hosea's explanation of their horrible situation attributed their loss and suffering to their own actions.

While it is often troubling for loved ones, self-blame can be an effective temporary coping skill for survivors that can help restore a sense of agency and empowerment to those who have suffered in situations over which they are powerless.[19] Part of being human and dealing with soul-wounding experiences is the drive to make sense of what has happened and to find meaning in the situation. In the case of ancient Israel, Yahweh's inaction was an intentional punishment. Yahweh had given them over to the consequences of their idolatrous and unjust behavior. Many of us are used to this theological orientation from Old Testament prophetic texts, but when thoughtful pastors, chaplains, and counselors hear it from people in the midst of suffering today, they typically discourage it. Naming this as a normal response in the sermon—for example in a section dealing with trouble—a preacher might talk about a traumatic event and say, "You may spend your waking hours running through the events of that day and imagine that you could have done something differently and prevented this."

The book of Ezekiel details the sins of the people that led to divine punishment through exile.[20] The shape of scripture here became more about faith in the midst of struggle and about living toward God's promises rather than the glories of the height of Israel's greatest monarchs. Ezekiel's words and strange behaviors may demonstrate the effects of trauma that the exiles were also experiencing. Particularly interesting is the prophet's "numb" behavior when his much-loved wife dies.[21] He doesn't mourn her, and he uses his response to her death as a metaphor for how the people will respond when Jerusalem falls.[22] Self-blame can be an intermediary step in the restoration of personhood and active human agency, but this does not always lead to experiences of healing.

Viewing self-blaming texts as a form of prayerful confession can be a helpful theological means to maintain a sense of human agency while moving on from self-blame toward releasing painful or wounding experiences into God's hands. To make this move in a sermon, a preacher may speak of the grace of releasing our past actions or inactions into the hands of God and give voice to God's response, "I hold all the days of your life in my hands. I forgive and love you."

It can be troubling to read prophetic texts through the lens of traumatized people trying to make sense of the horrible things that happened to them. Responsible pastors today recognize that not all the suffering that we experience can be attributed to specific sins. Remember the agonized conversations between Job, who insisted that he had done nothing to deserve suffering, and his friends, with their need to assign blame. Sometimes our actions can lead directly to suffering, such as texting while driving or having an affair that destroys a marriage, but much of the time it is futile to try to make a one-to-one link between our personal brokenness or shortcomings and catastrophes that cause suffering in our lives.

3. Focusing on the Power of God

Following the dynamic of assigning blame, soul-wounding experiences can be opportunities to focus our lives toward the one true God as Hosea did with Israel on the eve of destruction of the Northern Kingdom and exile from their homeland. David Carr calls wounding events "god-shredders" because they can provide an opportunity for believers to turn away from the many "gods" that exert gravity in our lives.[23] We can read scripture with an eye toward where God's power is in the text. In our sermons we can shift the focus from casting blame toward God, linking God's power with God's love so that even when God's action or seeming inaction confounds us we can rest in the love of God.

The soul-wounding experiences of the exiles have had a profound and deep effect on much of the Old Testament. The literate elites of Judean society had the skills, and may have felt pressing need, to record events and stories that had long been a part of the oral tradition.[24] While stories from Genesis likely existed in oral form, most scholarship agrees that it was compiled and edited following and during Judah's exile.[25] The original audience, survivors and descendants, "live with memories of war, physical dislocations, theological upheavals, and continuing doubts about their survival as a people."[26] Scholars largely see the stories in Genesis as hopeful in nature, although they also contain challenging theology and some violent imagery that shows the challenges and unfinished work of compilers who were still processing their experiences. Genesis is a book of beginnings for people who needed to begin again in the wake of disaster.[27]

The stories in Genesis can also be read as stories that emphasize God's power, which is sometimes displayed in challenging ways. For example, God punishes sinful humanity with the flood. As evidenced in the back and forth conversation with Abraham, God also wants to be fair to those who are living righteously in Sodom and Gomorrah. But the utter wickedness of the cities "forces" God's hand.[28] In Genesis 22, God tests Abraham's faith in what looks to be a cruel high-stakes game of "chicken," but Isaac is saved in the end as the God who demands also ultimately provides what is needed. As in the case of God's hand in the disasters in Genesis, God's provision in cases of barrenness, famine, and landlessness is offered in divine freedom. God does not always provide exactly what the ancestors, exiles, or we *think* we need. The exilic editors who lifted up these themes may have been working "pastorally" to sustain survivors in the wake of deeply wounding trauma.

Preachers may connect with listeners who carry soul wounds by looking behind the text and describing the history of texts such as Genesis. Because it was likely recorded by exiles who experienced intense trauma, preachers can talk about how interpretation and meaning-making is a part of healing from these events. This provides a way of dealing with some of the troubling theology in these passages. Preaching texts that highlight God's power and provision can sustain us today, particularly when preachers vary the stories they use when making application to our world. Doing this demonstrates that God's provision doesn't always come in the ways we might expect. Preachers will want to avoid endings that wrap up too neatly. Life rarely unfolds like a Hollywood movie. While we certainly want to preach hopeful sermons, those in our midst with fresh wounds keep us honest. For example, a miraculous birth may not happen for those struggling with infertility, but opportunities to serve as parents or parental figures may come through other means.

Finally, the extravagant promises of God in Genesis testify to the deep hope of early exilic editors. God's power to create the world out of nothing and to create again in the wake of disaster means that God can gather up the scattered and broken nation of Judah and make them a people again.[29] This same God can also bring healing and new life to broken people and situations today. God's promises to Abraham and his descendants surpass the threats they experience. God promises progeny as numerous as the stars, a safe and bountiful homeland, a name that will be remembered, and blessings that flow through Abraham's offspring to all the nations.[30] These abundant promises that emerge in the midst of barrenness provide a theological lattice for exiles making sense of their experience.[31]

4. Typology

Recounting biblical stories provided a means for survivors to process and make meaning from their experiences. Biblical accounts may not always be what we might call literal representations of the exiles' experience, but they do mirror that wounding experience in some significant typological ways. They are able to speak of long-ago violence, death, and loss in a way that holds those events at a safe distance.[32] These stories help make sense of what happened in the past and in the present. As Kathleen O'Connor notes, "Explanations, even wrong ones, stave off the sense that the world is absolutely, permanently chaotic."[33]

In sermons, biblical references to wounding experiences can extend a safe means of processing for survivors who may relate to wounded biblical figures as types of their own suffering, while also providing a window into trauma for listeners who have not experienced soul wounds. In chapter 4, I will demonstrate a typological approach that encourages wounded listeners to enfold their experiences into the Christ event through a sermon series based on the Apostles' Creed.

In the case of using typology as an interpretive tool, Genesis serves as an example with exiled Israelites modeling the healing potential in a way that preachers can use today. David Carr argues that their trauma was so recent and intense that they were not able to record their own experiences. They used Abraham, and his descendants, as a type, with his experiences serving as a stand-in for their own.[34] The lives of Abraham and his descendants are difficult—full of death, treachery, violence, and migration.[35] Their experiences are deeply relatable for exilic audiences and for listeners today. God's promises to Abraham are deeply comforting and function pastorally to nurture hope. Using Abraham as a type, exiles processed their experiences and found hope in God's provision, saving acts, and promises directed toward these ancestors of the faith. Carr notes the potent role of scriptural interpretation for trauma survivors: "It was a healing form of group memory. It was Bible for exiles."[36]

Preachers can utilize these texts in a similar manner today, allowing biblical figures to stand in as types for those who have suffered deep wounding experiences. The evocative power of preaching biblical figures as relatable ancestors of the faith means that pastors can refrain from naming explicit wounds that they know are present in the congregation. The lives of biblical figures provide a safe distance and buffer that allow for processing and meaning-making around trauma without reopening or irritating the tender places in listeners' lives.

As with Abraham, the life of Moses can also be explored as a typological stand-in for exiles seeking to process their own experiences and move toward healing and restoration. Moses seems to serve as a type for Israel as his own experiences foreshadow what will happen to Israel in Exodus events.[37] At times the depiction of God is troubling, but this too may reflect editors coming to terms with wounding and painful human experience. In an odd story in Exodus 4:24-26, God tries to kill Moses, who is saved when his wife, Zipporah, puts blood from their son's circumcision on Moses's legs.[38] Similarly, the firstborn of Israel are saved by blood on their doorposts while the firstborn of Egypt are killed by divine agency.[39] David Carr attributes the challenging theology surrounding God hardening Pharaoh's heart, the plagues, and God's delay in bringing Israel out of slavery as a typological parallel for the experience of exiles that ultimately testifies to God's care for Israel.[40] The Babylonian exile was long, spanning more than one generation.[41] Points of connection between Moses and Israel deepen the typological connection for exiles. Moses's experiences of provision and protection can be their story too.

Moses and the Exodus account are ultimately a story of survival and God's deliverance. The Judean exile officially ended in 538 BCE when Cyrus defeated the Babylonians, but it took many years for exiles to return or come to terms with their survival and new aspects of their identity.[42] The celebration of Passover can be understood in part as a way to work through and commemorate survival in a way that will pass on this experience to future generations.[43] The power of ritual and links to narrative heighten the ability of the Exodus to serve as a foundational pillar and stand-in for "exodus-type" experiences that will unfold for subsequent generations of Jewish people. It creates a sense of solidarity with those who have been delivered, whether or not those celebrating Passover today have experienced traumatic wounds or need to be delivered from something. While repetition and some forms of ritualization can be reminiscent of flashbacks that haunt some trauma survivors, ritual and memorialization can also be important aspects of coming to terms, integrating, and healing from traumatic events. The experiences of celebrating Passover for Jewish people and Communion for Christians can help the community support one another and come to terms with corporate wounds.

We can find a similar typological pattern in the New Testament. Early Christians used earlier scriptural figures as types to help process their own soul wounds. For example, they connected Jesus with Isaiah's suffering servant.[44] The figure of Moses may have also been a helpful type for the followers of Jesus when interpreting Jesus's death. Just as Moses "died on the threshold" of the promised land "so that his followers might move forward," Jesus died on the threshold of salvation so that his followers might move forward.[45] Both Moses and Jesus also lacked a known gravesite where later generations could pay homage.[46] Unlike other gospel accounts, Mark's original ending doesn't follow the resurrection with sightings of Jesus; instead, hope is found in the life of Jesus's community that continues and flourishes despite his horrific crucifixion.[47] For trauma survivors, life can be a vindication. Just as earlier scriptures brought meaning and hope to the early Christian community following Jesus's crucifixion, preaching scriptural events born of wounding experiences can be a part of fostering healing and resilience in listeners today.

5. *Cross and Resurrection*

While some biblical texts can be read typologically as a means of connecting with those who live with soul wounds, we can also read with an eye on deep hope connected to the death and resurrection of Jesus Christ that reaches through the biblical context to help sustain wounded people today.

It is hard to overestimate the role of the Apostle Paul in shaping Christianity. Paul had personal wounding experiences and wrote to communities who had also experienced trauma, yet his letters are also deeply hopeful and bear witness to the power of God to transform lives. Paul was known for supporting the persecution of Christians until Jesus Christ confronts him in a transformative event along the road to Damascus. Paul interprets his experience positively. He experiences salvation, healing, and a deep calling on his life as a result of encountering the crucified and risen Christ. There are aspects of his physical response to the event that are reminiscent of responses to trauma. Paul's letters don't tell us exactly what happened; however, the book of Acts describes Paul falling to the ground, being temporarily blind, and having an inability to eat or drink for several days.[48] Paul references his experience in his letters to Corinth and Galatia. It is clear that for Paul this experience divides his life into a clear "before" and "after," something that is common for survivors of significant trauma.[49] Theologically, Paul's experience is an early example of the broader Christian experience of salvation by dying and rising with Christ. While deeply life-changing, it did not cause a soul wound. However, his experience with a transformative rupture likely provided empathy for the new Christians he supported as they too navigated the changes spurred on by an encounter with Christ. While Paul was clearly still Jewish and followed the Law, his experience changed his relationship to the Law and inspired his commitment to bringing both Jews and Gentiles into a Jesus-empowered, faith-based relationship with God.[50]

The Damascus Road experience was positive, but Paul still struggled with wounding experiences in the midst of his ministry. Paul writes to the Corinthians and Galatians about some form of illness or personal weakness. He references a "thorn in the flesh," which others may have perceived as a hindrance or weakness for ministry.[51] Opponents also persecuted Paul through beatings, stoning, and imprisonment. Paul's own words in

2 Corinthians offer a brief account of his suffering in ministry.[52] Where others saw physical weakness and suffering as a detriment to his leadership ability, Paul's way of understanding the cross of Christ allowed him to turn weakness into strength in Christ and suffering into glory in Christ.[53] Paul enfolded his own experiences of suffering into the experience of Christ on the cross and saw this as a pattern to be followed by other Christians as he invited others to imitate him or follow his example. The way of the cross has become the way to live as a follower of Christ in a broken world. And the resurrection of Jesus places a boundary on suffering and nurtures faith. Preachers can follow Paul's lead by putting the cross and resurrection in conversation with traumatic wounds throughout scripture and in our world today.

Trauma-Informed Interpretation Example: Genesis 22

To demonstrate a trauma-sensitive approach to the Bible for preaching, I will explore the binding of Isaac from Genesis 22 at greater depth along with sermonic possibilities. The interpretive tools previously discussed are part of the exploration of the text. Many of the steps in the process are the same steps a preacher might typically follow when moving from biblical study to sermon creation. Genesis 22 is a foundational and challenging text for both the Jewish and the Christian traditions. In Jewish settings, this text is often referred to as "the binding of Isaac" or the *Aqedah*. In Christian settings we tend to refer to this text as "the sacrifice of Isaac." It is also a text that can pick at the edges of wounds that some in our congregations carry. Family members who experienced the death of their infant daughter named this text in particular as troubling. The idea that God would ask a parent to sacrifice a child is troubling to parents and those who may have experienced abuse or neglect as children. I have worked with pastors who rigorously avoid Genesis 22, which is a challenge as it is so important to the Christian tradition that it shows up twice in the Revised Common Lectionary: in the Easter Vigil and in the Ordinary Time texts for year A. In some other lectionaries, it also shows up in year B of Lent.

The pattern outlined below is not intended as a complete exegetical method but rather a supplement for preachers seeking to nurture possibilities for connection and healing for those with soul wounds.

Name What Troubles Us

Particularly when working with a challenging text, it can be helpful to list some of the issues this passage may raise for us or for our listeners. Part of preaching with awareness to soul wounds is looking for places where a passage may rub the raw places of human life. This is not a reason to avoid a text; rather, it can be an opportunity to bring comfort, companionship, and the possibility for healing. Here are some potentially troubling issues around Genesis 22.

- God tests Abraham after God has made a covenant with him and after Abraham has already shown faith.

- God asks Abraham to sacrifice a child, especially his beloved and long-awaited child of promise.

- Abraham says yes to this request! Some interpretive traditions hold that Abraham should have offered to sacrifice himself rather than his son.

- Why would God ask for this kind of violence?

- Where is Sarah? Are we to believe that Abraham received God's request, made preparations, and headed out on a journey without consulting with her at all? I would imagine that she might object!

- What does this text imply for our relationship with our own children?

- How might someone who has lost a child feel about this text? Why didn't God provide another "sacrifice" in their experience?

- Some listeners may bear wounds of neglect from childhood where they felt "sacrificed" on the altar of a parent or caregiver's choosing (career choices, addiction, other relationships, etc.).

- How does this passage change our overall perception of Abraham and his faith? How would it impact Abraham as a biblical figure if this story were absent from scripture?

- How does this experience change Abraham's relationship with God?

This is not a text for the faint of heart. This text calls us to roll up our interpretive sleeves and make some decisions as preachers as we wrestle to hear a word from God for our congregations and ourselves. Next let's move through the text to explore the structure and plot before utilizing trauma-aware interpretive tools from the first part of the chapter and discussing potential sermonic approaches.

Describing Structure, Movement, and Plot

Genesis 22 is set apart from the previous story of Abraham's covenant with Philistine leader Abimelech with the phrase "After these things…" and held together with a basic plot of the agonizing request that Abraham go on a journey to Moriah to sacrifice Isaac, resolved by the intervention of God's angel and the provision of a ram to serve as the sacrifice.

Walter Brueggemann explores this passage according to a pattern of calling and responding, which repeats three times.[54] The pattern of calling and responding is evocative for preaching because it frames Abraham's experience as relational and conversational. It echoes theologies and practices that undergird the preaching event. Abraham receives a Word from God that calls him to action.

1. God calls, Abraham responds, God requests sacrifice.

2. Isaac calls, Abraham responds, Isaac questions, Abraham answers.

3. Angel calls, Abraham responds, Angel resolves drama.

Section 1: Sacrificial Journey Initiated

God calls and Abraham responds simply, "Here I am," which is characteristic of Abraham. When called by God or other people, he responds without hesitation. The request that God makes to Abraham to take his beloved son, Isaac, and offer him as a burnt sacrifice to God is preceded with a participle "*na*," which some scholars think makes God's word more of a "please" request rather than a direct commandment.[55] Nevertheless, Abraham responds in obedience. He and his son prepare and embark on their journey.

While this may not have been the case for Abraham, to our modern imaginations, receiving such a troubling divine command may be traumatic or wounding in itself. We are tempted to think that our children belong to us, that we can keep them safe, and that we know what is best for them. Life can inflict deep soul wounds when we experience tragedy and loss. Those who experience a miscarriage or lost pregnancy feel betrayed when their own bodies couldn't protect their unborn babies. When a child of any age dies an untimely death from accident or illness, parents may carry deep wounds of helplessness, failure, and guilt.

Abraham takes wood for the offering and servants along with him. When they see their destination in the distance, Abraham tells the servants to stay behind. He and Isaac will continue on and worship when they reach their destination. Abraham tells the servants, "The boy and I will walk up there, worship, and then come back to you." Does his use of the plural illustrate his trust that God will not let any harm come to Isaac?

Section 2: Preparation for Sacrifice

Abraham places the wood on Isaac. It is troubling that the sacrificial victim must carry the wood that will incinerate his body. Jon Levenson points out the likely intentional connection with Abraham placing the wood on Isaac and his placing of bread, water, and the child Ishmael on Hagar's shoulder before turning her out.[56] Just as God intervenes and saves Ishmael and Hagar, so too will God intervene to protect Isaac. Abraham and Isaac walk along in silence, presumably each concerned with their own thoughts, hearing only the sounds of their footsteps. Later traditions will assign a sense of complicity to Isaac for carrying the wood, but this is not clear in the text. Levenson points out that we can easily imagine a young child simply carrying the wood as he has been instructed.[57] Isaac calls out to his father and breaks the silence, "Here is the fire and the wood, but where is the lamb for offering?" Abraham responds and answers Isaac's question in verse 8, which lies at the center of our pericope, "God will see to it."

Abraham's answer communicates deep trust in God amidst a potentially wounding experience and provides a solid theological anchor for this text.[58] The God who demands Abraham's most treasured son is the same God who can be trusted to provide everything. Neither Abraham, exiles who recorded or redacted this text, nor we can completely understand the ways of God. Nevertheless, we can trust God. Faith, resilience, and healing for wounded souls are forged in the midst of contradiction between what Brueggemann calls God's "dark command" and "high promise."[59] Our vision and power are limited and finite. In this text we move from a God who tests and demands to a God who provides.[60] For exiles and for wounded souls today, this passage offers a complex but deep hope.

Isaac and Abraham's journey continues to the place of sacrifice where the narrative quickly moves to a point of climax. All in verse 9 Abraham builds an altar, lays the wood in order, binds his son, and lays him on the altar on top of the wood.[61] We do not know why Abraham binds Isaac. Perhaps he is not a willing participant?[62] Alternately, this could simply be the pattern when offering a human sacrifice.[63] Then Abraham reaches out his hand and takes the knife to kill his son.

Section 3: Sacrifice Transformed

When an angel of the Lord cries out to Abraham, he answers again, "Here I am." The angel tells him not to lay a hand on the boy. Abraham has passed the test! Abraham looks up and sees a ram caught by his horns in a thicket: God has provided a sacrifice in the place of Abraham's son. Abraham names the place where all this occurs "The Lord Will Provide."

Having described the general movement of the passage, let's apply the five interpretive tools from the first part of this chapter to help us address some of the aspects of this text that trouble us.

Applying Trauma-Sensitive Interpretive Tools

1. Scripture as the Language of Faith

Reading scripture as the language of our faith encourages preachers to look at the language used in the text for places of resonance with wounded listeners as a means to nurture faith and relationship with God. If a preacher doesn't know the original language, it can be very helpful to use study tools or a commentary that highlights details that can be missed in translation.

The language in Genesis 22 reminds us that this is a story about a son. The term *son* is used repeatedly—some ten times, often with amplified meaning. Isaac is Abraham's son, his "only" or "favored" son, whom he loves.[64] The problem of Abraham needing an heir was a major theme in Genesis 15–21. Abraham has already sent his other son, Ishmael, out into the wilderness. In Genesis 22 Abraham now stands poised to offer his "promised" son, Isaac, back to God.[65] This is also the first time in the Old

Testament that we encounter the word for "loved" or "favored," used to further intensify the gravity of God's request.

The biblical language of "beloved son" is deeply resonant. For Abraham's sacrifice to God to be meaningful it must be something that he deeply loves. The doctrine of providence recognizes that everything comes from God. The idea behind firstfruits is that we give a portion of what God has given to us back to God. In this light, Abraham offers his son, who is a gift from God, back to God. Such giving acknowledges a posture of faithful dependence on God. This posture offered hope to wounded exiles and later inspired the author of the book of Hebrews and the Apostle Paul to lift up Abraham as a model of faithfulness to early Christians who were also enduring wounding experiences.

2. Assigning Blame

Modern interpreters have struggled particularly with the nature of God and God's test, which undergirds some of the most common concerns pastors and listeners name with this text. Is the excruciating agony of this test God's fault, or does the blame rest on Abraham or even Isaac for going along?

One of the troubling aspects of this text for many is that Abraham says yes to God's request. He doesn't challenge or even question that he should sacrifice Isaac. While we are told that this is a test, Abraham presumably doesn't know that.[66] We also know that Abraham is capable of bartering with God. He does so earlier concerning the fate of Sodom and Gomorrah. In the cultures in which Abraham lives, child sacrifice to a deity may have been common.

Isaac's age is also a concern for many. The word used to talk about Isaac could be applied to anyone from thirteen to thirty years of age. Isaac was not a passive child in these events. He likely had some agency although still under the authority of his father's house.

Concerning whether "blame" rests on Abraham, Kierkegaard's *Fear and Trembling* asks if good ethics can be suspended when following God's command.[67] Does the divine presence ever call individuals to make excruciating choices that fall outside of acceptable moral law? This is a dangerous line of questioning and one that certainly needs the presence and discernment of the community of faith. We may remember with horror accounts in the news from decades ago in which parents who suffered from mental illness killed their children supposedly in response to God.

Unfortunately, over the course of history and today, too many have sustained wounds associated with people mischaracterizing God's call. The next chapter will look at preaching healing words in light of the church's role as a complicit or active perpetrator of soul wounds. Such experiences may lead us to see the wisdom of Kant, who viewed Abraham as having failed God's test. Kant held that if a divine apparition called one to do something immoral no matter how "majestic the apparition may be and no matter how it may seem to surpass the whole of nature," the person must consider this command an illusion.[68] For Kant, moral law is an absolute. One can never be clear about whether the voice one hears is really God's.[69] As a fallible human, Abraham may have mischaracterized God's call.

3. Focus on the Power of God

One of the questions that troubles many with this text is why God tested Abraham. Testing happens in both the Old and New Testaments. Satan famously tests Job. Deuteronomy interprets Israel's experience in the wilderness as a kind of testing.[70] In the New Testament, Jesus himself is tested in the wilderness, and Jesus teaches us to pray that God would save us from the time of trial, temptation, or testing.[71] Early Christian communities experienced intense testing and may have wondered whether they could remain true to Christ in the context of persecution and pressure from surrounding cultural practices.[72]

Testing may be understood as an outcome of living in a world that has yet to fully experience the complete fulfillment of God's promise. God's reign is here but not yet complete. We must, like Abraham, accept the call that holds both God's testing and God's providence. If we seek providence without testing, we end up with what Dietrich Bonhoeffer calls "cheap grace." If we seek only testing, we refuse grace altogether. If we accept neither testing nor providence we find ourselves outside of covenant with God.[73]

Relationship with God means continuing to communicate, even in the aftermath of wounding experiences. In the same prayer that we pray about being tested, we also pray for God's provision. For those who are in the midst of a time of trial, prayer takes on a more urgent tone. We may ask God why we are experiencing this trial. We may ask God for assurance of survival or for God's presence to draw near to us.

It may be helpful to name the confounding nature of this passage in a sermon. We are creatures and cannot fully expect to understand the

Creator. God is large enough to handle our questions. Acknowledging that we don't have all the answers may be reassuring to listeners who are in the midst of trials. While our understanding has limits, we can still trust God. It is important to offer those who are suffering some secure theological footholds. For example, the unreasonable love of God is most acutely illustrated for Christians in the person of Jesus Christ, whose identity is marked both by crucifixion and resurrection, in whom we can lose ourselves and gain life.

Much of our focus so far has been on the risk taken by Abraham and Isaac, but some scholars emphasize that God too is taking a risk. This willingness to risk is part of God's power. Is Abraham trustworthy? God has promised that the covenant will be carried through Isaac. If Isaac is killed then God's promise will not be fulfilled. Risk-taking on God's part continues through all of scripture: in the incarnation, God embarks on a trajectory that will lead to risking God's own life in the person of Jesus Christ.

4. Typology

When dealing with a challenging passage, it can be helpful to remember that we are not the first people to read or preach this text. Genesis 22 has a rich interpretive history. We have named the theological resonance between this text and Jesus's crucifixion and resurrection. Early Christian interpreters saw it too and tended to interpret this text spiritually, in part as a way to deal with the difficulties of a more literal reading of the text. Irenaeus and Tertullian explored this text typologically, looking at the wood Isaac carried as corresponding to the wood of the cross. They saw resonance in the willingness of a father to sacrifice his son and found theological depth in God's provision—God providing the right sacrifice and the dynamic of God resolving the threat of death with life.[74] In one of the earliest surviving post-scriptural sermons, Melito of Sardis shows a significant limitation of this typological approach by noting that Isaac never suffers but Jesus does suffer.[75] Jesus goes further than Abraham and Isaac in obedience and faith.[76] Early Jewish scholars lifted up Isaac's willingness to die as an example for martyrs in the faith.[77] Sixteenth-century Christian Reformers tended to focus more on Abraham's faith than typological linking, but the use of this text in present-day Easter Vigil worship shows that the theological resonance continues to be important to the Christian tradition today.

5. Cross and Resurrection

The tool of seeking hope in the text by looking through the lens of Christ's death and resurrection is helpful for this passage. This text has deeply affected our atonement theology. In their book *Preaching the Atonement*, Peter Stevenson and Stephen Wright highlight several key points of resonance between Genesis 22 and Christ's atonement.

Obedience of Abraham and Jesus

Abraham's obedience to God up to the point of doing "the unthinkable" reminds us of Jesus's own obedience unto death. In the event of the crucifixion, God puts God's self to the same test as Abraham and proves God's deep and costly love for us.[78] That God experiences the loss of a child may be comforting to those carrying wounds of loss. This experience of loss is part of the life of God. We have a God who can intimately understand.

Unity of Father and Son

The closeness of Abraham and Isaac reminds us of the closeness of God and Jesus in the life of the Trinity, particularly the way Jesus and God are portrayed in John's Gospel as acting together.[79] Jesus leaves his disciples in the garden and travels the way of the cross without them, continuing on only in the presence of his Father, much the way Abraham and Isaac leave the servants behind and travel the last part of their journey alone. The unity in action between God and Jesus and the apparent closeness between Abraham and Isaac keep us from making Isaac a "pure victim" with no agency in this story and keep us from drawing clear lines of agency within the Trinity. The Trinity was working in concert rather than God the Father and the Son in antagonism.

The Ram and the Lamb

Here we experience contrast rather than similarity. Abraham and Isaac are spared the costly sacrifice because God provides what is needed. In the crucifixion God in Christ is not spared. However, we do see resonance between Isaac and Abraham and humanity; our theology proclaims that people are spared because of a sacrifice provided by God.[80] This claim may ring hollow for wounded listeners who have survived trauma. They may understandably ask why they were not spared from pain and loss.

Beloved One under Threat

The final point of resonance noted by Stevenson and Wright is the motif of a promised one—a long-awaited one becoming a victim. Isaac isn't only a beloved son, although this is clear in the text. Behind this text is the story of God's promises, God's covenant with Abraham and

Abraham's descendants, and, ultimately, God's blessings for the nations. God's promises are bound up in Isaac. We can imagine that this may have felt like a burden for Isaac. Some in our congregations may resonate with the wounds connected to high expectations, especially people who experienced loss in childhood like Isaac did.[81] Jesus too is the long-awaited Messiah of promise yet paradoxically dies so that God's realm can come and God's life-giving purposes can be fulfilled.[82] As followers of Christ, we too are called to give up everything so that our lives can be given back to us in freedom.[83]

Having engaged our interpretive tools, next we will move to options for creating a sermon on Genesis 22.

Sermonic Options

When dealing with a challenging text like this, the preacher needs to have a sense of the wounds that might be touched or triggered and how listeners may respond. In the immediate aftermath of my sister-in-law's sudden death, my father-in-law and mother-in-law were unable to navigate their well-meaning friends at church. They didn't want to talk to others about what had happened. When they were able to return to church, they were very sensitive to anything in the sermon that would relate in any way to Twila's death.

For a text like Genesis 22, it may be helpful to focus more directly on the text. For example, the threat of Abraham losing Isaac, especially when Abraham has already sent Ishmael away, is tragic. Those who have lost children or come close to losing children will be able to supply their own life experiences here without naming this explicitly in application sections of the sermon.[84] The use of theological shaping is still crucial here, and God's provision in the face of loss can become a framework for those who are struggling to make meaning.

For those who have experienced recent wounds, preachers may want to allow the biblical figure to typologically "stand in" for the wounded listener and avoid making an explicit reference to wounding experiences in our world today. In order for the text to feel vivid and serve as a "stand-in," preachers will want to use accessible language to create empathetic connections, making the biblical figures relatable. Using the biblical narrative rather than a present-day story of children under threat allows those with raw wounds to go at their own pace and use the biblical figures as "stand-ins" to process and make meaning from a safer distance.

At other times listeners may crave honesty surrounding wounding experiences. Listeners who have received wounds at the hands of their parents or caregivers may feel a lifting of shame as they find typological resonance with Isaac's experience in this text. One of my preaching students focused on God's liberating power and used Isaac as a type for those in bondage today as she chose to preach about God's provision for Isaac and celebrate Isaac's survival in the sermon.[85] She preached against much of the broader Christian tradition by naming problematic or challenging aspects of Abraham's character. Stressing that perhaps God needed to test Abraham given that he had previously lied, had failed to trust God, and had sent Hagar and Ishmael away to certain death in the wilderness. While it was linked to telling the truth about child abuse, listeners to this student sermon encouraged care with the vividness of imagining Isaac's experience of being bound. The text does not tell us whether Isaac struggled, but the image of a parent overpowering a child was a triggering image for some listeners.

Preachers may want to name challenges and troubles raised by this text in their sermons to validate the response of listeners. Wounded listeners don't want easy answers. They need nurturing for development of a robust faith that can handle real challenges. Caring and pastorally sensitive preachers will find ways to address the challenges and questions raised from this text while also helping listeners experience this text as life-giving rather than mainly troubling.

Another sermonic approach is to explore the challenges of this text from more than one angle. This was a tactic employed by Jesus in his own parables. Things are not always what they seem, which allows for a sense of paradox that grants listeners deeper insight into this passage and their own lives. The use of transitions like "look again" or "if we take another look..." can prepare listeners for this move. With this pattern the text becomes a multifaceted jewel that we can explore from more than one angle. This approach can also work with a theological grammar that moves from human need to God's provision. For example, the initial trouble in the text may be that it appears that Isaac's death is needed. A deeper look may expose broader cultural practices of child sacrifice that would lead Abraham to not question the divine command. The move to grace is not only that God provides what is needed for the ritual of sacrifice but also that God subverts a terrible cultural pattern. Unlike other "deities," Yahweh does not require the ritual death of children.

Conclusions

Scripture bears witness to wounding experiences and shows us that God not only heals but also uses people who have been wounded. This brings a sense of purpose and meaning for those who have suffered and survived. To facilitate God's healing, preachers can employ trauma-specific interpretive tools as part of a broader exegetical process. Showing connections between present wounding experiences and biblical figures gives survivors language to process their pain and grow in faith. Using biblical language directly in parts of our sermon that attend to our world today helps the Bible feel less remote and more relevant for listeners.

Recognizing traumatic experiences that form the historical context of those who recorded or redacted parts of the Bible help us understand some of the ways that God is characterized. In addition to "blaming" God, these texts also often blame Israel for their situation. Sinful actions such as idolatry, poor leadership, and failure to keep the law explain why God has given them over to their enemies. Employing blame as an interpretive tool doesn't mean you don't have faith. This can be a helpful response as part of a healing process. God is big enough to handle it. It is not a preacher's responsibility to "get God off the hook." Preachers can normalize the response of self-blame while gently moving listeners through prayerful confession and release.

Preachers need to stay in close communication with those who carry deep wounds. Preaching is not a separate act from pastoral care. In a sermon that uses a deep theological grammar, there is a place for truth-telling about the horrors of human brokenness. When someone's world is falling apart, it naturally elicits strong emotions. God is strong enough to handle these emotions. Sermons that take God's healing power seriously must tell the truth about the deepest pain so that God in Christ can redeem even this pain. At times, it may be helpful to stick more closely to the biblical text and allow the experiences of biblical figures to "stand in" for the experiences of listeners without making painful links that are too concrete for listeners' wounds. For preachers who are seeking to nurture resilient congregations, the biblical text can provide a window to speak truthfully about the wounds that individuals and communities carry and God's healing power.

Chapter 3 now turns to equipping preachers with techniques that can facilitate healing for wounds that may involve church leaders or church institutions either by direct action or by inaction. I will also discuss the resistance some listeners may experience around addressing these wounds.

Chapter 3
Soul Wounds in the Church

In a book that focuses on how the church and preaching in particular can be a part of God's healing of traumatic wounds, we must look at wounds the church has at times inadvertently inflicted upon others. Preaching can be an integral part of facilitating healing for the church and for those harmed by the church's actions or inactions. A strong leader can help individuals and groups move toward healing by helping survivors feel safe; by disrupting corrupt, abusive, or violent cycles; and by gathering groups of support within a congregation.[1] Sermons can actively support these ministries.

The church has caused and deepened wounds in a variety of ways. A church leader with gifts for ministry can simultaneously be deeply broken and act in sinful, illegal, and wounding ways. The church has also acted collectively in ways that have wounded individuals and groups. Racism, sexism, colonialism, participation in cultural genocide, anti-Semitism, and complicity in the face of clergy sexual abuse are examples of traumatic wounds caused in part by or deepened by the church. God has redeemed the church as the body of Christ, but congregations are still composed of people and are subject to the promise and peril associated with being human. Actions that harm another also create a reciprocal wound in the perpetrator, linking both groups in a painful dance.

While these wounds might not impact every church member directly, the church's corporate witness has been hurt by wounding behaviors that have recently come to light. In past generations, people may have automatically trusted a member of the clergy. This is no longer the case. Recent decades have brought scandals surrounding clergy sexual abuse across most denominations. Systemic cover-ups are well known, highlighted in the Net-flix series *The Keepers* and Oscar-winning film *Spotlight.* Denominations have negotiated legal and financial settlements associated with abuse and cultural trauma caused to indigenous peoples, and megachurch pastors have been charged with financial mismanagement and fraud.

Trauma is a wound that threatens the ability of an organism to func-tion; God offers the church healing and the opportunity to be a witness to God's love in a wounded world. Our Christian witness is unified and strengthened when we face our collective wounding behaviors, change prac-tices, and seek forgiveness. The scars that remain can serve as generative reminders, much like the scars on the hands and feet of the crucified and risen Christ.

Some in our congregations may feel a desire for justice for survivors of wounds caused or deepened by the church leaders or structures, while oth-ers resist acknowledging these wounds and simply want to move forward. Being in relationship with those who carry wounds from trauma is difficult. It can be draining and time-consuming. It can be painful for pastors—who love the church and who have given their lives to its service—to learn about the damage that other congregations, church structures, past practices, or leaders have caused. While it can be complex to walk alongside those with soul wounds connected to the church, God's justice and sanctifying grace urge us on.

This chapter explores how the church has caused or contributed to traumatic wounds and offers suggestions for preachers seeking to support healing. As with the other chapters, principles offered here may be useful to preaching that fosters healing for many experiences of pain and brokenness and for pastors who desire to be sensitive to the needs of diverse listeners. What makes this chapter different is its attention to the dynamics pres-ent when the church has contributed to or deepened a traumatic wound. While the church has contributed to a range of wounds, the issue of sexual abuse in the church has been particularly shrouded in shame and has not been effectively addressed in regular congregational worship contexts. In a recent entry on Our Stories Untold, a website oriented around support for survivors, one of the moderators discusses the challenges facing survivors and communities of faith:

> The other day, my colleagues and I were reflecting on the sense of angst we have when folks in communities of faith ask us for examples of people getting it right when it comes to responding to abuse.... The problem is, we don't know of many success stories to tell. Partly, that's because

they're shockingly uncommon. In my years of talking and hanging out and working with survivors of sexual violence, I can count on one hand the number who have been satisfied with the way their reports of violence were handled. Just kidding! I can count them on no hands, because zero is the number of sexual violence survivors who have ever said to me anything remotely close to that.[2]

Using the wound of sexual abuse in the church as an example that could be applied to other wounding situations, I will explore resistance often expressed by congregations and church institutions in addressing wounds. The discussion will then turn to specific dynamics associated with the wound of sexual abuse in the church and options for preachers that address these dynamics in order to facilitate God's healing for the church and survivors. A sample sermon demonstrates one attempt to put these techniques to work.

While the wound of sexual abuse is raised as an example here, the preaching suggestions are applicable to any situation where the church at some level has acknowledged its role in causing or intensifying soul wounds. Preaching that supports healing from wounds related to the church is usually most fruitful when the preacher has some support from other leaders either in the congregation or in broader denominational structures.

Many Factors Contribute to Resistance

It seems like the same story has been told again and again in different venues and forms: A vulnerable person is abused by a Christian leader in a position of power, the systems around that leader close ranks and protect the leader, and the abuse continues.[3] Recently my own Mennonite tradition has had to face mishandling of abusive behavior of our best-known theologian, John Howard Yoder, toward women throughout his career, including female students while he served at a Mennonite seminary.[4] Yoder never denied the charges and was disciplined by suspension of ministerial credentials. However, the suspension did not affect his academic pursuits or associations, including a term as the president of the Society of Christian Ethics in the late 1980s. Yoder's abuse came at a time when Mennonite women were just beginning to be ordained as pastors, and there were fewer women than men in Mennonite seminaries. Not only were these survivors abused by a male professor, they were also hampered by a broader church culture in which women in leadership were viewed as suspect. While Yoder did officially experience a disciplinary process and was asked to leave the Mennonite seminary where he taught, many victims didn't feel acknowledged because he continued to teach elsewhere, lecture, and publish widely. It seemed that the abuse was spoken about quietly to protect Yoder's reputation. Further, Yoder didn't really acknowledge that his own behavior toward these women was wrong. When traumatic pain is not dealt with, it does not go away; rather, that pain often becomes part of violent cycles that play out in the lives of survivors.[5]

It is painful to acknowledge a pattern of wounding that has been pervasive in the church. Such behavior is markedly at odds with biblical teaching from both the Old and New Testaments that promote God's love and special care for the most vulnerable members of our communities. While survivors of abuse in a church or Christian context understandably tend to become critics of the church, other members and even witnesses to abuse may express resistance that can affect preachers seeking to facilitate healing around this issue.

Resistance from Conflicting Loyalties

Witnesses to sexual abuse in the church often feel caught in a terrible bind. Judith Herman, professor of psychiatry emerita at Harvard, addresses the agony of dealing with traumatic wounds caused by other people. "When the events are natural disasters or 'acts of God,' those who bear witness readily sympathize with the victim, but when the traumatic events are of human design, those who bear witness are caught in the conflict between victim and perpetrator. It is morally impossible to remain neutral in this conflict. The bystander is forced to take sides."[6] This dynamic is especially challenging in a church context where members may experience a sense of loyalty toward an accused leader *and* victim or victims. Even years later, preachers may encounter resistance to preaching about unhealed corporate wounds that stir listeners to make an active choice around what would bring healing or justice for the situation.

Unfortunately, the easiest response for most church members caught in the midst of abuse allegations is to take the side of the perpetrator by doing nothing.[7] It is very difficult to overcome the power of inertia. Often we allow life to just unfold around us without intervening. Herman writes, "[The perpetrator] appeals to the universal desire to see, hear, and speak no evil. The victim, on the contrary, asks the bystander to share the burden of pain. The victim demands action, engagement, and remembering."[8]

Accused leaders complicate witnesses' perception of the truth with alternative explanations: "It never happened; the victim lies; the victim exaggerates; the victim brought it upon herself; and, in any case, it is time to forget the past and move on."[9] The more power a perpetrator has, the more difficult it is to unravel this line of reasoning and the perpetrator's prerogative to control the narrative that "defines reality."[10] When a witness or bystander encounters evidence of abuse without a narrative web to make sense of it or without a community to support or confirm, the easiest course of action is to simply "look the other way."[11] Herman notes that this pattern holds even if the victim is an "idealized and valued member of society."[12] This phenomenon is visible in the allegations brought forth by well-known figures such as Professor Anita Hill, more recently by music artists Kesha Sebert and Taylor Swift, and by numerous famous actresses who have accused Harvey Weinstein of assault. It follows that when a victim or victims are already on the margins or considered less important, negative response or lack of response essentially relegates the abusive experience outside the bounds of accepted reality.[13] Herman writes, "Her experience becomes unspeakable."[14]

Preaching can help by opening the possibility of another narrative, one that courageously speaks a difficult truth. Simply naming the abuse and brokenness has the potential to make invisible realities visible and to bring a sense of credibility and humanity to victims who have been sitting quietly in the shadows. Through the power of the Holy Spirit, preachers can harness words to bring life.

Resistance because Truth Is Incompatible with Identity

Churches do tremendous good in our world but have also allowed leaders and structures to harm some vulnerable members. Churches aspire to the highest of virtues, actually being the hands and feet of Jesus Christ in our world. Churches comprise good people, God's "saints" on journeys of sanctification. We are simultaneously saved and sinners, composed of both dust and the very breath of God. It is very hard for an institution with a core identity built around doing good to acknowledge, repent, and change when it has done something evil. We are human, and by God's grace we do participate in God's redemptive mission toward our world. This is the identity we proclaim. Nevertheless, every church or church institution has aspects of who it is that are at odds with who it professes to be.

Congregations and other virtuous institutions may deny harm to protect the supposed good being done, even if the harm is eating away at the souls of victims and bystanders.[15] This may feel like the best course of action initially in order to keep strong ministries going and avoid disruption in effective church programs and outreach ventures. However, not only does denial create the possibility that more victims will be harmed, but a culture of denial eats away at the whole congregation's witness to the truth, which hurts the credibility of the church over time and creates barriers to mission in the community.

In their essay "Virtue and the Organizational Shadow: Exploring False Innocence and the Paradoxes of Power," Maureen O'Hara and Aftab Omer discuss the challenges faced by altruistic institutions when leaders or institutional structures cause harm to others.[16] Their claim is that evil enters institutions when there is a significant gap between the good the institution thinks it is doing and the harm it may actually be doing.[17] On the other hand, if the reality of harm outweighs and undermines the perceived good that a church or organization is doing, why should such an institution exist? The risk is annihilation.[18] Allegations of abuse leveled at pastors who were perceived as effective leaders can lead to them being fired. Congregations doing vital ministry can be sidelined by understandable questions of identity and purpose.

Broader North American culture is known for amnesia around cruel or negative behavior. Numerous figures have enjoyed a "second act" following serious allegations of abuse, including Hollywood icons Woody Allen and Roman Polanski. This "amnesia" compounds the challenges facing altruistic organizations that may harm others while aspiring to help.[19]

To keep a sense of identity and purpose, churches and other organizations may resort to extreme actions to defend a myth of innocence. For those who work in churches or church institutions, work is more than a job.[20] Our work represents what is most precious and important to us.[21] Our defenses against perceived attacks have generated systems of "gatekeeping" and denial that have at times affected preaching and hurt people who have already been victimized.

According to O'Hara and Omer's research, groups have collective defensive strategies that they employ—often without being completely aware of them.[22] They are psychological, cultural, and structural.[23] They are embedded into our congregational patterns, leadership models, and polity; our written church discipline materials and procedures; and even our worship and preaching. The most basic responses are "simple lies, distortions of fact, or spin" often followed by "cover-ups" and "blame shifting."[24] Once we know what we are looking for, we can see this behavior at play in nearly every sex abuse scandal that has rocked our denominations. Allegations are made, and church members and other leaders don't believe the victim.

They want to protect the accused until they have "proof." The perpetrator lies and covers up behavior. Supporters spin the story: "It wasn't sexual assault. . . . It was a consensual relationship." Or, rather than acknowledging that abuse happened to a teenager by her youth pastor or Sunday school teacher, supporters may emphasize that the girl was eighteen and legally not a minor. They may emphasize aspects of her attire or behavior, naming that her attraction to the youth pastor makes her partially responsible. Churches want to focus on reforming and forgiving perpetrators and don't want to acknowledge that they have been lied to. Strategic communication keeps the full story of what happened from being reported in broader media. Conferences don't want to deal with the problem, and so they sign off on transferring an accused pastor from one region to another. Victims are told, "He will never serve in a church again." Perpetrators are told, "These allegations will never see the light of day." Finally, those with power write the official histories of our congregations and denominations so that the chosen narrative is maintained and victims are "erased."[25]

Resistance Silences Victims and Disrupts Healing

Churches and church institutions mistakenly think that they can attend to abuse and discrimination "in-house," that these are concerns of sin and immorality when in fact these are violations of the law and need to involve official channels and legal systems outside of the church. Too often leaders have preached for victims to forgive or not seek "earthly justice." These behaviors have a silencing effect on others who have experienced abuse and send ripples of pain through entire systems. The inertia of bystanders and disempowered witnesses allows broken behaviors and practices to continue.

Victims struggle to find ways to heal.[26] Discontinuity between the calling of a church or pastor and abusive behavior is deeply wounding. Like bystanders who cannot connect the dots because the abusive behavior deviates so far from expected behavior, survivors may have a very hard time integrating what happened to them. When someone experiences a crisis in his or her family, they may go to a pastor for support. When a pastor is the abuser, the victim may not know where to turn. Because the system has put forth a false myth of the perpetrator's innocence to protect itself, the victim/survivor often turns to self-blame rather than "acknowledge the helplessness and powerlessness that comes with victimization at the hands of those whom they have loved or admired."[27]

Unpacking some reasons behind resistance in no way excuses the church's behavior toward survivors, but it does help us understand in part why it has happened and why resistance continues. By growing in awareness we may be able to shine the light of Christ into our impulses, actions, and inaction, and change how we relate to survivors. Church leaders, congregations, and institutions are finite and imperfect. We live with knowledge of past brokenness and a readiness to confess to our harmful actions or failure to act. Church leaders and institutions can also begin to see survivors in our midst not as "tokens" representing an easily dismissed alternative perspective on the behavior of the church in the world but as holy witnesses empowered by the Spirit to help us see ourselves more clearly so that we can change our behaviors and grow more in Christ's likeness. If survivors' voices are valued, the church can combat the myth of false allegation that plagues survivors of assault and abuse in other contexts.

Sexual Abuse in the Church Causes Deep Wounds

Many pastors have never and will never have a church member approach them to talk about an experience of abuse in the church, and consequently, they may assume that this is not a wound that affects their congregation.[28] Unfortunately, this is simply not the case. The truth is that there are likely survivors, current victims, perpetrators, and a host of bystanders listening to our sermons on Sunday morning. When a wound is unaddressed, time does little to help. Even if abuse occurred in a congregation decades ago, wounds may still need God's healing. Like other wounds the church may experience, sexual abuse can harm the entire community.

While the presence of survivors in church can indicate that they have already experienced significant healing, the church's discomfort and resistance to engage with abuse risk deepening their wounds. Marie Fortune names several reasons survivors may hesitate to talk to their pastors, including a fear of being judged or stigmatized; a sense that the pastor is not professionally, spiritually, or emotionally equipped to receive this information; or discomfort with being vulnerable with a male pastor if the abuser was male and vice versa.[29]

An associate pastor recently survived a crisis in her congregation where the lead pastor covered up abuse involving a former Sunday school teacher. Later it was revealed that the lead pastor had left his own trail of sexually abusive relationships across several church conferences. The associate pastor recounted her anger at his preaching as these events came to light. This pastor used the pulpit to justify his actions, twisted biblical texts, and cast blame upon the congregation rather than accepting responsibility for his own actions. For example, he preached about Jesus's teaching against judgment and pointing out the speck in a neighbor's eye in Matthew 7 to mean that the members of the congregation should refrain from critical discernment and official action around the behavior of the pastor in this situation.

Congregations trust pastors. This is part of what makes a preaching relationship so powerful. In cases of sexual abuse and misconduct, preaching offers a public venue for a pastor who has broken the law and the trust of the congregation to continue spinning a web of lies. These behaviors are a poison that affect every area of ministry. Like putting drops of dye in water, no part of the water remains clear. It follows that the preaching ministry of a pastor is impacted by abuses carried out in a counseling or care context. Because the consequences of an abusive breach are so severe, a pastor's need to protect himself or herself and control the narrative takes precedence in the pulpit even over the gospel. It destroys a preacher's ability to look at the text and the congregation with clear eyes. When a pastor who has harmed a church member takes advantage of the authority and sense of authenticity that comes with the office of pastor and uses it not to bear witness to the gospel but to continue to harm others, he or she must be removed from his or her position immediately.

When abuse occurs in a church, those who uncover the abuse need to seek outside support from a lawyer, the police, or an organization such as Dove's Nest, Faith Trust Institute, or the Survivors Network of those abused by Priests (SNAP). This is challenging because churches want to forgive. They don't want structures that impede genuine relationships, but having clear leadership accountability in place can prevent abuse and can give a congregation a clear path for dealing with it.[30]

Congregations struggle in the wake of a pastoral breach of conduct. Many in the church want to put these events behind them and move forward, but when trauma is not addressed, it does not go away. Congregations experience complex emotions that may be helpful to acknowledge in preaching. Some in the church may feel grief at the loss of who they thought their pastor was and betrayal that the church was a place of wounding rather than a locus of God's healing. Some may experience anger toward victims because their painful experiences brought the crisis to the fore. Victims often feel betrayed, unwelcome, and eventually angry at the church for not intervening earlier.

Pastors preach to the whole congregation and need to find ways to attend to complex and conflicting emotions. Placing responsibility on the former leader who violated the law and the trust of the congregation can stop a culture of finger-pointing within the church. Preachers can also helpfully steer the whole church toward truth-telling and growth. Trauma that has been addressed can strengthen future resilience. God's healing can make us stronger at the places where we have been broken.

Preaching to Those Who Have Been Wounded by the Church

In a sermon preached at the Cathedral of St. John the Divine less than a year after the September 11 attacks, Fr. Michael Lapsley offered three categories for reflection in the wake of trauma: "What was done to me (us), What I (we) did to others, what I (we) failed to do."[31] These questions may be helpful for people in various postures surrounding soul wounds in the church. The answers to these questions may serve as an indictment for the church.

The sad truth is that many recipients and survivors of church-inflicted wounds are no longer part of the church. For these people, being in church would be equivalent to a battered person remaining with an abusive spouse. To remain in the church is to risk complete loss of self. The survivors who continue to wrestle with the church in the wake of wounding are often those for whom the church is extremely important, including those who may be called to ministry. For survivors who remain with the church, theological questions may emerge as deeply important in the wake of trauma, at the same level as medical or psychological care.[32] In spite of past harm perpetrated, by God's grace survivors do come to church to seek hope and signs of transformation. In preaching to those with wounds caused by the church, the following approaches may contribute to God's healing for listeners.

Listen

Listening is the first step to preaching that facilitates healing, especially when the church has been involved in wounding. People who have been hurt by the church often feel betrayed because the church is called to exemplify God's love. This is not the time to offer excuses for leaders or institutional structures.

"Coming out" as a survivor of trauma can be both difficult and empowering. Survivors may fear that they will be discounted or taken less seriously. However, telling one's story can bring strength and hope as secrets and shame are brought into the open. Pastors will want to listen to what survivors need to feel safe and to come to a place of healing. Preachers will want to avoid simplistic therapeutic responses such as "God will take care of it in God's time" or "Forgive and forget."[33] These filler statements function, at best, as jargon and sail right through listeners without making an impact; at worst they may be seen as not taking survivors' wounds seriously or as letting perpetrators off the hook.

If a survivor has shared her or his story with the pastor, these can inform an approach to preaching and worship without betraying confidences. For example, if certain stories or language would trigger trauma symptoms for a listener, the pastor can plan worship accordingly. At one of the churches where he served, my husband guarded survivors in the congregation by editing a video that mentioned rape occurring in a country where the congregation was financially supporting relief work. The video's power and message were clear without the reference, and survivors in the congregation were cared for. Another simple approach is to give a survivor advanced warning if there is something in the biblical text or sermon that may stir up old wounds—perhaps even allowing her or him to see relevant parts of the sermon in advance.

The Holy Spirit serves as guide and comforter for preachers in their work of listening and responding through advocacy and consolation. It is troubling to hear stories of brokenness and pain caused by the church. Pastors feel a deep commitment to the church. When the pain is more than we can bear, the same Spirit that upholds survivors upholds us in our vocation. Wherever the church has sinned and not lived up to God's intentions, the wounded Spirit of God stands in the rift to provide strength, support, advocacy, and comfort. The Apostle Paul tells us that the Spirit's language is deeper than words; however, the same Spirit also animates proclamation and empowers listeners to respond.[34]

Preaching as Caring for People

A good sermon is structured and intentional, engages both biblical text or topic and the context of the sermon, and communicates a central theme that places God's redemptive and hope-filled action at the center. That said, some effective models of preaching can tend to feel more "task-oriented" than "people-oriented." We design our sermons with our theme sentence, a vision of what we hope the sermon will do, and/or a problem we hope the sermon will address. These methods have a proven track record and are part of how we evaluate good preaching. For most of us, these approaches are meaningful. We encounter Christ and experience grace.

In a similar vein, pastors and other church leaders sometimes tend to approach situations of brokenness and injustice as tasks that need to be handled or fixed so that the church can move forward with other matters. Preaching about justice issues can feel like a checklist a preacher may be internally marking as part of socially responsible ministry. In a broken world, there is no end to these tasks, but in our rush to solve problems, we may be rushing past the humanity of those directly involved. For example, we may seek to address the problem of hunger by donating food without actually engaging with those who are hungry. While directives can help a church move forward in ministry and bring concreteness to preaching, people who have been harmed by the church are not merely a problem to be solved. Preachers need to create space for the full humanity of the wounded.

Preachers acknowledge humanity by using stories and examples that avoid stereotypes and easy answers. True stories that have already been widely published, stories told in a way that protects anonymity, or stories told with permission carry more freight than made-up stories, which can sometimes be dismissed by listeners struggling with resistance.

Preachers may want to experiment with collaborative approaches to biblical interpretation and proclamation. Preachers can still preach a structured gospel word of hope, but incorporating more voices in the process may be healing for people whose voices have been excluded or silenced. Besides collaborating in sermon preparation, congregations can provide opportunities for members to offer testimony or respond to the sermon, either in the worship service or through social media.

Being honest about our limitations opens doors where offering absolute answers may close off channels for further communication and relationship. It may be helpful for preachers to say phrases such as "This trouble is deep," "I don't have all the answers," "God's healing is not yet complete," and "We wait and pray in hope." Being honest about our limitations can be a helpful step early in our sermon preparation process. As we move forward with questions of the text and contextual concerns, and set out a central theme and hopeful action for the sermon, it may be beneficial to hold these goals or tasks lightly. God may have other purposes. Envision the arms of God holding you, your congregation, and any newcomers or visitors to worship in a deep embrace. God holds what we cannot hold, and we can release our deepest intentions into God's care.

Confess and Apologize

Acknowledging the failures of the church is healing not only for survivors but also for the latent communal wounds that were caused by cover-ups, denial, and brokenness in the system.[35] Anger is a natural and common response for those who have experienced trauma, as is the need to experience some sense of justice. Abusive and wounding behavior is wrong. When the perpetrator is connected to the church, following discernment and support from the congregation and broader denominational structures, representatives of the church may be able to step in with words of confession and actions of reparation.

For example, about a decade ago, Lutherans issued an official apology to Anabaptist denominations, of which my own Mennonite tradition is a part, for persecution during the sixteenth-century Protestant Reformation. The lead-up to the formal apology by the Lutheran World Federation acknowledged that Anabaptists harbored a deep sense of pain around Lutheran persecution, killings, and torture during the reformation.[36] This formal apology from Lutherans to Anabaptists is only one such apology that Christian denominations or groups have issued to those who have been hurt or wronged by the church in the past. Southern Baptists, United Methodists, Roman Catholics, and the Episcopal Church have all apologized for racism and racist behaviors. Numerous denominations have also formally apologized to indigenous peoples. In 2007, the Canadian government oversaw a massive financial settlement to be paid by Catholics, Anglicans, the United Church of Canada, and Presbyterians to descendants and survivors of religious settlement schools. Preachers can cite these official acts of apology in sermons as signs of God's healing in our midst.

While the context of a church institution is different from a congregation and may not be immediately transferable, preachers can learn from processes and practices undertaken by church institutions. Decades after John Howard Yoder abused women students at the Mennonite seminary in Elkhart, Indiana, in March 2015 the faculty, administration, and board of Anabaptist Mennonite Biblical Seminary (AMBS) gathered for a reunion weekend of worship and listening to each other. Victims had a chance to speak and to meet with administrators. The current president, Sara Wenger Shenk, offered a formal confession and apology for the mistakes in the system that allowed Yoder to continue harming women.[37]

In addition to the confession and apology, preaching and worship were important for the witness of the church, for showing support, and for offering validation to the women Yoder abused. The seminary planned two worship services. The first was invitation-only, primarily oriented toward those who had been harmed by Yoder. The second service was open to the public. In her public sermon, "The Year of the Lord's Favor," Wenger Shenk built on themes of her confession and apology statement. She used Isaiah 61:1-4 to name the deep violence and brokenness of sexual violence alongside the power of God in Jesus Christ to rebuild and restore following destruction and loss. She said of sexual violence, "It's an insidious, stealthy, often invisible devastation that creeps in to dismantle lives, destroy reputations, shatter families, and poison entire communities with its ruination."[38] She also sought to empower and inspire survivors by naming those who have been broken and oppressed as the very ones who will do the rebuilding Isaiah declares in the wake of devastation.[39] Next she moved to the New Testament where Jesus quotes this text in the synagogue in Nazareth. Jesus was endangered for suggesting that the religious leaders and powers of the time may not have everything figured out according to the realm of God. The inability of the leaders to see what Jesus was trying to show led to more devastation.[40] She quoted Jesus's lament over the city of Jerusalem and offered lament as a way forward for leaders today who have also failed to see.[41] She ended by focusing on Jesus's loving desire to gather all under his wings. In their brokenness, AMBS leaders want to be gathered up along with survivors to receive Jesus's healing and restoration so that together they might give glory to God.[42] Wenger Shenk's boldness in calling out present-day leaders, empowering the witness of survivors, and seeking reconciliation and healing as a means of glorifying God serves as a testimony that can contribute to the very reconciliation, restoration, and healing that she seeks and serves as an example for other preachers.

Wenger Shenk and others from AMBS acknowledged mistakes made by earlier administrators in confronting Yoder's abusive behavior in an empathetic manner that didn't cast blame. If a former pastor or leader is scapegoated, that restricts future pastors and leaders—potentially causing them to close themselves off. Elders, pastor-congregation relations committees, organizational boards, and denominational structures can help discourage and protect leaders from being scapegoated.[43] We don't want a power vacuum where administrators or pastors can't be leaders out of fear of being blamed for institutional sin.[44]

Preachers are representatives of the church, even when we don't agree with all the actions of broader institutional bodies in the church and even if we were not involved in wounding actions. With broad congregational support, the use of confession and apology in worship and preaching may help facilitate healing for wounded listeners.

Embrace Nontraditional Worship Spaces and Diverse Metaphors for God

The wounded Spirit of God calls us to God's healing through comfort and advocacy, which has implications for worship and preaching. The physical space of the church may be a trigger for some survivors; listening to sermons online may be the closest they can come to participating in public worship. As we prepare our sermons, it can be helpful to remember that we may not see all listeners and that the Holy Spirit may use our words to minister to a survivor we may never meet.

Varying the metaphors that we use for God in our preaching increases the ways that our listeners can connect to God. Years ago, I had the privilege of walking alongside a seminary student who had experienced trauma in a church context. Traditional church practices and language triggered serious responses in both seminary and church contexts. In part, this student found healing and connection to God through the divine feminine Spirit of God and by using feminine language to address God. Working with this student served as a reminder to me that gendered language in worship can make a difference for survivors of abuse.

Beyond language and metaphor, many denominations have created liturgies specifically for worship with survivors of abuse. As part of this project, I spoke with survivors of abuse in a church context and those who work with survivors. Many named Communion as a challenging liturgy. The language around sacrifice can sometimes be twisted to lift up our own sacrifice as somehow redemptive, particularly if an abuser is the one officiating. In a context where someone has been deeply hurt, it may be impossible to receive the gift of Communion through a traditional liturgy. A team from my own denomination, Mennonite Church USA, took two years to design an alternative Communion liturgy that is sensitive to the experiences of those healing from sexual abuse. The group presents the liturgy as one for regular use rather than for a "special" service. Among other practices, during the passing of the peace the new liturgy suggests placing palms together and gesturing forward in acknowledgment rather than hugging or shaking hands to protect survivors from a trigger through unwanted or invasive touch.[45]

Preach about Justice

Many survivors express a need for justice as part of healing.[46] Unfortunately, when preaching about justice, we tend to talk about it in distant rather than personal terms. On the other hand, in conversations with those whom the church has wounded, the topic of forgiveness is common. This favorite Christian topic and tenet that lies at the heart of atonement theology and in our celebration of Communion has frequently been problematic for survivors who feel that this word flows easily off the tongues of those who haven't been hurt. Too often the heavy lifting is left to be done by the wounded rather than condemning abusive behavior from the pulpit.

Every congregation has victims/survivors and likely perpetrators of abuse. One advocate encouraged me to imagine a twelve-year-old girl being sexually abused by her uncle, a child who has told no one what is happening to her, as one listening to my sermons. What is the gospel for this child of God? Wounded listeners need to be reminded that the abuse is not their fault—that it was wrong, that they are loved by God—and validated by naming abusive behavior as evil. Further, we can trust God to hold forgiveness as a gift and promise rather than a burden to be thrust on those who have suffered injustices. As one survivor pointed out to me, even Jesus said "*Father,* forgive them." We can place in God's hands that which we cannot do.

Preaching can also contribute to justice for survivors. In broader culture, revenge is often confused for justice. Marie Fortune encourages a focus on vindication rather than revenge.[47] While revenge can perpetuate cycles of violence that create new victims, vindication is more of an experience of deep acknowledgment and liberation. Sermons can contribute to vindication by speaking up for victims and witnesses who may have been silenced by institutional inaction. Advocating and organizing both real and symbolic actions can bring a sense of restoration to survivors who may feel alienated or cut off from others in their pain.[48] When the church has contributed to injustice, the church needs to offer steps toward justice by reaching out to those who have been harmed. Often these events and actions may take place in situations other than worship services, but preaching can support these measures. For example, mentioning from the pulpit that a church is having a retreat that will address experiences of abuse by a past leader legitimizes that event. Preachers can emphasize that the gospel offers liberation to those who are bound by past experiences. For survivors this liberation may involve receiving greater power, whereas for institutions or leaders who have harmed others, their power may be curtailed.

The Bible is a powerful resource for preaching justice to survivors. Scripture contains numerous instances where religious leaders and institutions failed to protect all of God's people. We can read these texts with an eye to how the church has failed today. Naming this in the sermon allows for God to bring healing to both survivors and institutional failure. Marie Fortune offers this revision/interpretation of Psalm 146:8-9:

> God sets the rape victim free and opens the eyes of the powers-that-be.
> God lifts up those who are bowed down and loves those who seek justice.
> God watches over children and upholds the victim and survivor, but the way of those who cause harm to others, God brings to ruin.[49]

Preaching with an eye toward justice for survivors does not mean that we can't also preach forgiveness. One survivor who serves in a congregation with other survivors speaks about the importance of forgiving oneself. Many survivors blame themselves for the abuse they suffer. This is especially a challenge with abuse in the context of the church because a perpetrator may be perceived as one who is "doing so much good" or as a "representative of God." The victim/survivor may feel that the fault lies in them rather than in the church leader. Further, the church as a system has tended to protect perpetrators and invalidate the experience of survivors, which leads survivors to doubt their own perceptions and wonder, "What is wrong with me, that everyone else supports the perpetrator's story?" Forgiving oneself can help survivors move from cycles of violence in their lives to healing and productivity. Preaching about God's love for them can be a first step in unraveling harmful patterns of self-blame.

Preaching Can Uproot Secrets and Shame

Preaching can bring words to that which has been forced into silence. Secrets allow wounds to deepen and isolate victims/survivors, which fosters shame, fear, and hopelessness.[50] Being open about abuse from a position of authority in the church helps remove the stigma that many survivors experience. Preachers can give voice to victims/survivors whose voices have been silenced or co-opted. Preachers don't need to focus on abuse every Sunday but can name these hurts as trouble regularly in sermons.

Preachers can also specifically name the church's role in causing or deepening wounds. Some preachers are afraid to bring up this "dirty laundry" in front of newcomers and visitors, but the truth is that these people will learn what happened soon enough through church gossip or back-channel communication. Even if it remains unspoken, newcomers can still see wounded behaviors, such as troubled relationships, and a lack of trust that may remain in the wake of a wounding experience.

Perpetrators and the systems that surround them create powerful narratives of denial that perpetuate "the way things are" at the expense of people who have courageously come forward to report abuse. Preaching can participate in a corrective narrative that tells the truth about the pain caused to survivors. As in all good preaching, it is important that our words invite listeners into a "world"; in this case, the world of one whom the church has wounded. The tools of plot and description can help listeners understand the depth of pain caused and their own role in it. This naming of trouble also opens up opportunities for bearing witness to the ways that God is present, brings healing and hope, corrects broken systems, and reforms the church. Yet, in creating a corrective narrative, preachers should resist moving too quickly to the good news. God's grace can be expressed in fragmentary ways that acknowledge the slow process of healing and the challenges faced by survivors.

Avoiding Violence and Stereotyping in Preaching

Many sermons oriented toward engaging with the sins of abuse utilize vivid and heart-rending stories to help listeners understand the deep pain survivors experience and carry with them. Preachers should exercise great caution in telling troubling stories in sermons. Details of violence can harm listeners and insidiously overpower the good news. Preachers should avoid using profanity or describing violent scenes graphically in sermons. It can help to test such material with a trusted group of church leaders, friends, or a pastor peer group. While we want to encourage empathy for those who are hurting, we also want to avoid emotional manipulation.

Before using a story about abuse, it can be helpful to provide a "trigger warning." One of my students employed a warning like this before preaching about David and Bathsheba in preaching class. In our feedback conversation, some commented that they appreciated the warning so that those who had a history of assault, rape, or sexual abuse could internally prepare. Others received the warning with energy because they knew that this sermon was going to "get real" about the pain and wounds caused by sexual assault and the abuse of power. In a congregational context, preachers could provide a trigger warning a week in advance and post something on a church website or Facebook page.

Judith Herman writes about the challenges faced by survivors and their loved ones in reconstructing a meaningful narrative:

Reconstructing the trauma story also includes systematic review of the meaning of the event, both to the patient and to the important people in her life. The traumatic event challenges ordinary people to become a theologian, a philosopher, and a jurist. The survivor is called upon to articulate the values and beliefs that she once held and that the trauma destroyed. She stands mute before the emptiness of evil, feeling the insufficiency of any known system of explanation. Survivors of atrocity of every age and every culture come to a point in their testimony where all questions are reduced to one, spoken more in bewilderment than in outrage: Why? The answer is beyond human understanding.[51]

Preachers are theologians who are called to stand in the breach with those struggling to understand. Constructing a theological narrative that moves redemptively from death to life in the sermon can help listeners see God's healing and empowering work as a new narrative that reconstructs the earlier narrative of trauma and powerlessness. We are empowered by the wounded Spirit of God and invited to bring words to the struggle and to help with the long, slow process of helping survivors make meaning from meaninglessness.

While clearly naming evil acts as evil, preachers should still take care when talking about people, whether in the Bible, prominent public figures, or people groups. A "good versus evil" or "us versus them" narrative can lead to dehumanizing or even demonizing others, which can justify violent or vengeful actions as a response to wounding.[52] Sermons should avoid caricatures and stereotyping people from the biblical text and our world. Showing empathy to everyone, even those who have made grave mistakes or engaged in sinful behaviors, more honestly reflects the complexity of our world where good people can make very bad decisions and ultimately, despite our worst and costliest decisions, can still be redeemed by God.

Often those with deep soul wounds have developed their own narratives that allow them to survive in a broken system or make sense of what happened to them. For example, a person who was abused by a pastor and experienced the church as resistant and caring more about maintenance than justice or the well-being of victims may live according to a narrative that all Christians are hypocrites. A person with a wound fueled by this narrative is unlikely to visit a church. If survivors are present in worship, it shows that God has already brought significant healing.[53]

When pastors start being open about abuse in sermons, people may come up after the sermon to talk. They may share about their own wounds. It may be helpful to talk about plans to discuss abuse with elders or deacons in advance, to set up care teams or support circles, and have information for referrals available. This is not a time to "go it alone." Leadership may find it helpful to prayerfully discern goals and a plan—a sense of vision around this issue. Judith Herman echoes something that has been repeated by survivors I interviewed. Saying something, speaking up, or "coming out" as a survivor of abuse is a crucial step in the healing process.[54] When a church has been the source of wounding, being able to share this experience in a church may be a particularly powerful step along a path toward healing.

Naming Grief and Diverse Perspectives in the Sermon

Naming the wrong, and the church's complicity in it, inevitably leads to a sense of loss and deep grief. We mourn the loss of our former picture of the church leader or institution. We mourn a loss in relationships when leaders are removed from a position—even if we know that the leader must be removed.

Even when the loss is necessary, it is still appropriate to name the many losses associated with traumatic wounds in the church. Naming losses is sensitive and is best done with awareness of the different perspectives in a congregation, such as from those who experienced abuse directly to those who only recently learned of the abuse. A congregation may have those who still feel a sense of loyalty to a previous leader. A pastor is called to preach to all of these people. Just as we cannot "refer away" our preaching ministry to those with deep soul wounds, we also cannot abdicate from our preaching ministry to those who find themselves on different sides of a church abuse scandal.

Representing diverse perspectives in the pulpit and challenging prevailing beliefs that hold the congregation together can be helpful in the wake of trauma. Engagement with diverse perspectives actually grows resiliency and empowers a church to deal with it when something bad happens.[55] "Practices that support creative conflict within an organization bring to the surface key differences that can serve to expand an organization's capacity for problem solving and wise action" and help erase "false solidarity."[56] It may also be helpful to invite voices from outside: a consultant, trauma-informed guest preachers, pulpit exchange with a church with membership representing minority communities, and so forth.[57] Our sermons should obviously respect human dignity, but experiencing shame is not always a bad thing—particularly for those with power and privilege. These experiences can be part of our journey to sanctification.[58]

Developing a shared hermeneutic and involving the community in developing a shared narrative about the traumatic events that incorporates diverse perspectives can contribute to healing for the whole congregation.[59] Part of debunking the "myths" that allow abuse to continue in church structures and church institutions means being realistic—even with shining the bright light of reform. Honesty involves living in the real world rather than an idealized world. Most organizations, even churches, can't be completely transparent about all things. O'Hara and Omer astutely note, "Responsible stewardship of organizational power entails discretion about facts and even intentions."[60] Demanding complete transparency in all institutional or congregational leadership practices is naive and not helpful for organizational or congregational functioning.

A crisis of sexual abuse by a leader is deeply painful and harms the church's collective witness. However, these deep sins and wounds as well as many other expressions and experiences of pain and brokenness are not fatal to the church or its calling in our world. With the uncovering of these harmful practices, we are in a time of transformation for the church, a season where there may be more openness to diverse perspectives and creativity, where our beliefs about ourselves can be rightly questioned.[61] If congregations and church structures can view this season as an opportunity, the church can emerge as a better witness for God's healing intentions for creation. Evil is not something that is just "out there" beyond the walls of the church; it is in us too. We can't view ourselves as innocent of wounding behaviors. By acknowledging limitations, terrible mistakes, "vulnerability and finitude," congregations and church institutions can serve as humble and discerning leaders in God's healing work.[62]

A Sample Sermon: "Defanging the Snakes"[63]

Text: Numbers 21:4-9

Google is full of suggestions to help you find a missing snake. Apparently snakes are both masters of escape and of staying hidden. No matter how tight the cage seems, snakes can find a way out. All of these websites were clear. If your snake is missing, don't panic; your first job is to find it—a hard task as snakes can remain hidden for months, even years before resurfacing when you least expect it.

A lost snake can be more than a hassle for a panicked pet owner. Several years ago a python in a pet store escaped its cage and traveled through the ventilation system to kill two young boys sleeping in the apartment above. A former employee recoiled in shock and disbelief: the cage had two locks on it![64]

Thinking that we have something under control doesn't mean that it is under control. That which is hidden can suddenly emerge like a snake to bite us when we least expect it, which brings us to the situation of Israel in our text today.

God's people are wandering in the wilderness. The book of Numbers is a book about people who are on the move from slavery to freedom. Through the lens of the experience of these people we learn again and again that your body can move to a new situation but your insides—that is, your heart, your mind, and your spirit—can lag far behind. God has freed Israel from bondage, travels with them, and cares for them, yet deep within are the hidden barbs of slavery, mistrust, fear, anger, and fixation on scarcity. Wounds of slavery hidden and festering on the inside, rising to the surface in moments of weakness or stress.

Numbers is a complex book with many types of literature and a lack of scholarly consensus around a chronology of the events. Yet it is marked by the repeated surfacing of the wounds of slavery. Israel is often ungrateful and grumbling, fearful and mistrusting of leadership. Leaders make poor choices and suffer wrenching consequences. One scholar names the "central tragedy" of Numbers as an inability to move forward and live into the liberation that God has promised them.[65] In chapters 13 and 14 they stand on the verge of the Promised Land, longing for Egypt and wishing they had died as slaves. And so God decides that they are not yet ready. They will spend forty more years in the wilderness learning and healing with God before their children will enter the land.

One of many episodes where Israel's wounds rise to the surface happens in Numbers 21 when they are in fact making their way again toward God's Promised Land. In the verses just before our reading for today, Israel is granted a resounding military victory over a Canaanite king, a victory so complete that they rename the place where the victory happened "destruction." Yet here, just verses later, the people are complaining. Why did God bring them out of the security of Egypt? As slaves they had no freedom, but at least they had food and water. They complain about the food—first saying there is no food and then, like a tired child who doesn't like the options in the refrigerator, whining, "There's nothing to eat."

As a result of their complaining, they experience a plague of poisonous snakes. Snakes lurking under the blankets in their tents, snakes hiding in the brush where they collect kindling for fires, hidden snakes suddenly jumping out to bite ankles and toes, poisoning them with venom that spreads quickly. The text tells us that many Israelites died.

That which is hidden has become lethal—whether wounds of slavery that poison the promise of a future with God or venomous snakes lurking in their camp striking out with bites of death.

That which is hidden in our lives can also be lethal. Memories and secrets buried deep inside, locked like snakes in the cages of our hearts can escape and attack. We don't always see the enemy coming when it is buried down deep inside us.

I recently read about a young woman who had experienced many years of sexual abuse at the hands of different abusers—some trusted family friends and others church leaders.[66] Her memories are full of holes, empty spaces where youth service trips and evenings playing at a friend's house should be. These memories are so painful that her subconscious is protecting her, but she still feels their effects—panic attacks, depression, anger, and fear. At fourteen she became pregnant through rape. In fear of her rapist, she carried this secret and had to also endure the judgment of her church community that demanded that she repent of her sin of sex before marriage.

Because her experiences were hidden in fear, even her parents and other loved ones were unable to help her. Hidden, they had control over her life. Like lethal snakes these secrets lay waiting for moments of stress and weakness to attack. Her abuse manifested in physical illness and symptoms as well as emotional pain and insomnia.

Recent news events reflect similar dynamics in the worlds of Hollywood and Washington, DC, powerful men who abused women and were protected by a culture of secrecy.

Abuse can also happen to men and boys, but women and girls are socialized with unique vulnerabilities and throughout our world have too often become the keepers of terrible secrets, secrets that threaten from within.

So often in the church we have tended to focus on sin as something active—something that we do. But what about sin that is done to us? When we are sinned against we also become containers for that sin. Dr. Park has described this kind of sin as compressed energy—it lies coiled like a hiding snake beneath the surface of life, draining away joy and hope.[67]

But just when the snakes threaten to do us in, God steps in. God's love is relentlessly committed to liberation—for our bodies and also our insides, liberation from that which threatens to kill us from the inside out. God defangs and deactivates the snakes in our lives.

No matter what Israel does, God sticks with them—hidden wounds, fear, and fatigue are no match for God. In our text, we expect God to remove the snakes, just as God has tangibly provided food and safety in the past. But in wisdom, God chooses another way. In fear the people turned to Moses, who falls on his knees before God in prayer. God responds, asking Moses to construct a bronze serpent and put it on a pole. When someone is bitten by a snake, they can look at the serpent on a pole and live.

God takes that which is hidden and lethal and deactivates it. He defangs the snakes by bringing them out into the open—setting them up on a pole for all to see.

When those who have been bitten by snakes look up at the bronze serpent, they live.

One scholar notes that God provides the healing in this text but that individuals need to take some action to receive it—they need to look up, they need to claim the healing God has provided as their own.[68]

In our gospel text from John, Jesus compares himself to the snake on a pole.

Jesus too will be lifted up, and through Jesus God deactivates sin. All the sins—the deeply hidden sins: the things that we have done, the things that were done to us.

All these sins are defanged, drained of their power. Christ is destroying the power of sin in our lives. God is defanging the snakes!

When secrets are revealed, that which was once lethal becomes power for new life. God is defanging the snakes.

Naming the thing that hurts us can lead to healing; it can no longer threaten to jump out and bite us. In naming it can no longer exert secret and deadly control over us. We name it into the light of God who is overturning the power of that which enslaves or kills us. God is defanging the snakes.

A young woman can say, "I was raped." A college student can say, "The discipline that my parents used on me was actually abuse, and it wasn't my fault." God is defanging those snakes.

The "me too" movement has brought validation and solidarity for many women who carried the secret of sexual abuse. Bringing these secrets to light also invites allies like a modern-day Moses to intercede, to help those still caught in the clutches of secret snakes. God is defanging the snakes!

Whether we shout from a hilltop or publish online, bringing hidden wounds into the light of Christ offers a chance for healing. God is defanging the snakes!

That which was once a hidden shame becomes a point of witness. God is defanging the snakes!

The young girl who experienced so much abuse stands tall today as a survivor. She rejects the shame of the sins committed against her. God is defanging the snakes!

Her life is a testimony to the sustaining and healing power of Jesus Christ.

God is defanging the snakes!

In the name of Christ, I say to you today: Whatever was done to you, it was not your fault. The power of Christ casts out this evil; it can no longer harm you.

Jesus Christ is a vanquisher of secrets and pain that snake around our hearts and souls. He takes on the pain and brokenness of these hidden wounds in our lives. Turning to Christ gives us courage to bring that which is hidden out into the open where it loses its power over us forever and we can experience complete freedom. God has defanged all the snakes!

In a few moments we will gather together to share Communion. At the Lord's Table we are welcomed as we really are. There are no secrets, no shame, and of course no snakes at this table. At this table, the power of sin has been defanged, and we experience a foretaste of healing, wholeness, and complete freedom in Christ.

Sermon Notes

I preached this sermon at United Theological Seminary, attending to the dynamics of the season of Lent as well as having been asked to speak about a topic that would focus specifically on women. While a seminary setting is different than a congregation, I was still able to utilize many of the techniques discussed in this chapter.

Part of writing this book entailed interviews and conversations with people who have been wounded by the church, and some experienced sexual abuse in a church context. In the past, students have also shared wounding experiences. These conversations, prayerful study, and the worship culture at the seminary allowed me to foreground the sermon as a means of caring for wounded listeners rather than primarily teaching or seeking to persuade the listeners. This is not a mutually exclusive choice—sermons can do many things—but it helps focus the sermon when preachers have a primary aim in mind.

The seminary itself is a nontraditional worship space, and we livestream worship services on Facebook, which makes sermons widely available. I crafted the sermon with the awareness that my listeners would not all be present in the chapel.

By explicitly talking about the harmful power of hidden things and naming God's action as liberation from hidden things that enslave us, I sought to uproot the pull of the secret and shame of sexual abuse. My descriptions and story in the first half of the sermon named secrets as part of the trouble. When I moved to healing in the second half of the sermon, the good news was focused on God's action of removing the power of these hidden "snakes" rather than erasing the pain experienced by those who had suffered abuse. God's liberation moves in the direction of justice, freeing them to move toward healing and wholeness. Nevertheless, this is a long journey and I avoided providing easy answers or too tidy an ending. The move to Communion following the sermon brought Christ's presence intimately into our midst in a way that offered an eschatological foretaste of complete healing.

The website that published the story about the young woman who had endured many years of abuse used horrific details in part so that the writer would not feel shame and not have to self-censor after doing so for many years while also leaving no doubt in the readers about the nature of the abuse.[69] For the sermon, I took care in sharing the narrative so as to name abuse clearly but not trigger traumatic responses or give violence a means to take hold of listeners' attention. I also avoided stereotyping the people of Israel as "ungrateful" with a more sympathetic interpretation of their collective behavior. While I did not offer a "trigger" warning for listeners, the worship leader did give mention of the work I had been doing around trauma at the start of the service. I also alerted the worship coordinator and dean of the chapel in advance so that they would be prepared to pray with students or offer anointing during our celebration of Communion or after worship.

Chapter 4 will feature many more sermon examples and approaches for preaching that promotes healing from soul wounds and strengthening the resilience of the church for participation in God's healing mission toward the world.

Chapter 4

Healing for
Wounded Souls

I n a small Texas town a man with a gun entered a church during worship and fired off hundreds of rounds of ammunition, killing twenty-six worshippers ranging from a young toddler to senior citizens. In addition to regular worshippers, among the dead was that Sunday's preacher, who served as an associate pastor at the church, as well as a couple visiting that congregation for the first time. In a world where our churches can be scenes of death and injury and where media images replay heart-wrenching interviews of stunned survivors, what can we say? While those who survived the shooting and immediate friends and families of victims certainly experience more intense trauma, when an event like this happens, we all feel the effects. Closer to home, about twenty-four hours before this mass shooting, a fifteen-year-old member of a congregation in a town near our church was killed when a drunk driver slammed into her car at a high speed. Local, national, and global traumatic experiences impact us, and the effects can accumulate in our bodies and souls.

In the midst of serious trauma and other more common wounding experiences, preachers can help. As agents of grace we can contribute to God's healing for those with soul wounds. We can also foster resiliency in our congregations so that they can better weather the storms of faith and life and emerge as powerful witnesses to God's activity in our world.

This chapter begins with a discussion of how preaching can deepen listeners' experience of the gospel and nurture congregational resilience. I will then offer a buffet of possible approaches and examples of preaching that can foster God's healing, starting with preaching in the immediate aftermath of a wounding event and moving outward toward preaching as a means of healing and broader Christian formation, exemplified by a sermon series focused on the Holy Spirit's reconstruction of the self through preaching the life of Jesus as outlined in the Apostles' Creed. Listeners who are deeply formed according to the life of Christ are equipped with theological faith tools to face life and minister to others in a wounding world.

Preaching the Gospel Builds Resilience

The Healing Power of the Gospel

When wounds threaten to take over, listeners need to experience the presence of the God who receives our wounds, embraces us with healing, and transforms hopelessness and loss into a meaningful life and future. Wounded listeners keep us preachers honest about brokenness in our world and the challenges of feeling connected to God and others in the wake of loss. However, our sacred calling as preachers pulls us beyond brokenness toward God's real presence in our world and stitches together the places where the fabric of life has torn.

It can be tempting for pastors to spend energy explaining or defending God's seeming inaction in the wake of a horrific event. We may do this as a way to channel our emotions into a cerebral safe zone or from our genuine concern to offer solid constructive theology in a deeply formative moment. However, God does not need our protection. Anger at God can be a natural and helpful response to trauma, and can maintain and even energize relationship. God is large enough to receive our anger, to safely and securely hold it so that it doesn't harm others or us.

Experiences of powerlessness, hopelessness, and isolation that can follow a traumatic event or set of prolonged traumatic circumstances mean that particular aspects of gospel or good news may need to be lifted up to speak to particular needs. For example, preaching about the presence of Christ in the midst of suffering and the Christian community as the body of Christ reminds survivors that they are not alone. Preaching a sense of reliance on the Holy Spirit when one's own power is insufficient offers empowerment in Christ and hope in the promises of God.[1]

Following my sister-in-law Twila's death, I needed to repeatedly hear the proclamation of Easter, that Christ is risen, to counter this experience of death that looked and felt so definitive. My memories of her and my carefully constructed theological footholds for navigating life were powerfully shaken by shock, tragic details around her death, and her sudden absence. I longed to hear about Jesus's resurrection and experience assurance that death neither holds nor lastingly defines Twila or any of us. Christ's move from cross to resurrection serves as a promise of our own move from death to life and can be experienced fragmentarily in our world today—in part through experiences of surviving, healing, or finding new purpose in the wake of trauma. Preaching the gospel can be a counterbalance, a check on our wounded perspective. The good news of the resurrection never gets old or tiresome, and listeners struggling with wounds of all kinds need to hear it.

Wounding experiences can permanently change survivors, but this does not mean there is an absence of the gospel. Healing will likely not look like a return to indiscriminate optimism. Serene Jones puts it this way:

> For those who are able to move forward and experience some degree of healing from traumatically inflicted harms, it seldom happens in a direct, linear manner and the past from which they are recovering never completely leaves them; it is never vanquished. This means that in lived experience, most survivors are never completely made anew and thereby restored to the self they were before harm found them.[2]

More common is that survivors find a way to manage, function, affirm life, grow, and trust others.[3] In the wake of wounding experiences, survival and a return to life among the living can be celebrated as a manifestation of the gospel in our sermons. Gospel experienced as provisional or partial, a foretaste of greater and deeper healing and joy found in God's horizon, is still good news for listeners with a range of painful experiences.

Resilience Guards People from the Power of Soul Wounds

Resilience in the face of a wounding event is rooted in early life experiences but can also be aided by supportive, caring relationships and guidance by trauma-aware leaders. It can be helpful for pastors and other caregivers to remember that simply surviving a deeply wounding or traumatic experience shows extreme resilience; the challenge can be unlearning the coping mechanisms that allowed one to survive a horrific experience in order to engage with ordinary life again.[4] When a wounded person comes to church, it is a sign of God's healing presence nurturing resilience and growing a desire to connect with others and to believe in Christ. No matter how deep the wounds, simply showing up merits celebration and praise to God. I remember the words of the old spiritual, "You know my soul look back and wonder, how did I make it over."

Preaching that participates in God's healing for wounded listeners helps break cycles of violence and nurtures faith and skills that can help people embrace life again. When a person is caught in a violent cycle where wounds continue to exercise control over life either through self-destruction or harming others, it can feel like the wounded person is trapped in a kind of prison. The wound or wounding event has more power than it deserves. God can liberate us from the tyranny of old wounds and brokenness. Conditions that can encourage survivors to "break free" include safety, support from others, guidance in managing physiological symptoms, and regaining a sense of "body/brain regulation, leadership, and choices."[5] The role of leadership is especially significant for preachers. When a community or individual is in crisis, the brain does not function fully or efficiently. Pastors can help guide people spiritually and morally so that they can live by their values during seasons where a traumatic wound may be interfering with a sense of identity.[6] Preachers can remind listeners who they are in Christ and emphasize the hope and core of our faith. This is why proclaiming the gospel *kerygma* is so central to funeral services.

Once the wound no longer has a vice-like hold on the soul, mind, and body, there are numerous tools that can help foster healing, restoration, and resilience. These tools are not sequential. Healing is often an incremental process with ebbs and flows; it doesn't follow a straight path. People may revisit these tools as needed.

Acknowledge the Wounding Event

Trauma specialists group a number of behaviors and actions under the umbrella term *acknowledgment*.[7] Allowing space for mourning and grief over what has been lost in both the wounding event and in the time following can help release pent-up physical, emotional, and spiritual energy. Grief can be named and normalized in the sermon. Preachers can be up front about their own grief as well as grief present in the biblical text. The Psalms offer examples of deep grief; so too do numerous biblical narratives. The sermon can also memorialize, which is often done instinctually in funeral sermons. The sermon can remember and name what is lost as well as use naming rituals connected to the loss.

Create a Ritual

Rituals can be very important to both individuals and communities.[8] A ritual in worship need not be complex. Lighting a candle, inviting members to come forward, kneeling, bringing a concrete memento or representation of the loss or wounds, and holding a moment of silence can all be helpful components of a healing ritual.

Tell the Story

Storytelling can also be deeply restorative.[9] It validates and strengthens the one whose story is told. The story and the interpretive frame around the story both can help survivors make meaning from trauma. The importance of interpretation is just one reason it can be beneficial for preachers to put stories into their own words rather than reading directly from a book or showing a video clip. In a setting where the focus is on healing from wounds, preachers will want to make full use of setting their own interpretive structure so that it is appropriate to their context. An alternative pattern would be to read or quote the words of one who is in the midst of healing, with permission. The sermon will still frame the storytelling, but this will allow marginalized voices to come to the fore.

Along with telling the story of the one who is wounded and healing, preachers can also engage with the stories of those who may have contributed to causing wounds.[10] Quaker peace activist Gene Knudsen Hoffman reminds us, "An enemy is someone whose story we haven't heard."[11] Of course, we need not tell every story in the sermon, but it can be helpful to expand a congregation's perspective after survivors are well on their way to healing. Telling the stories of perpetrators in sermons may be met with resistance, but this too may be part of the healing experience. Hearing the other side in a story helps survivors make meaning by showing the roots of violent behavior, uncovering bias, challenging "us-them" thinking, and re-humanizing our enemy, which can help end scapegoating behavior.[12] Even with all these benefits, telling a story about a perpetrator of violence from either the biblical text or our world in a sympathetic way will likely disturb or upset those who are victims of violence. Preachers will need to attend to the specific wounds of the congregation when making choices about what stories to tell and when to tell them. Engaging with stories, both our own and those of our "enemies," is a form of risk-taking that actually creates new neural pathways in our brain that contribute to healing and new life.[13]

Preaching Words That Heal

Preaching in the Wounding Moment

Preaching that attends to fresh wounds doesn't always have the luxury of being tempered by days of study and careful "word-smithing." When I talked to preachers about their experiences of preaching following a traumatic event, many remembered not being able to preach the sermon they had originally prepared and being compelled to preach something fresh that dealt with the crisis at hand. A survey of sermons written in response to local or broader traumatic events shows sermons that are timely and pastoral but not the best or most eloquent sermons ever preached. These sermons were not created for later reflection but are preached "along the way" in the midst of an unfolding experience. Not being perfectionistic about the sermon and occasionally allowing the "seams" to show can be more invitational to members with messy lives. In the immediate wake of local or broader traumatic events, listeners would rather have a relevant word that speaks to what is happening in our world than a perfect and well-researched sermon.

Voice and Language Support Healing in Survivors

Sermons that incorporate experiential elements to connect to emotions may speak more deeply to survivors. Physician, professor, and director of the Trauma Center in Brookline, MA, Bessel van der Kolk explores the body's role in healing trauma. Brain scans of trauma survivors show that these experiences shut down the parts of the brain that impact speech and light up parts of the brain that register images.[14] Further, the experience of flashbacks deactivates the left brain, which is more oriented toward language, logic, and sequence; and energizes the right brain, which is more intuitive, emotional, and experiential. Van der Kolk notes that the right side of the brain is more influenced by expression, body language, and primal human sounds such as singing, swearing, crying, and mimicking.[15]

At the risk of oversimplifying complex brain function, we need both halves of our brain to function properly. We experience life through the right side and use the left side to explain, put experience to order, and make sense of life.[16] When something triggers a traumatic memory or response, the right side acts automatically as if the event is happening in the present.[17]

Because the left side is deactivated, it is nearly impossible for the traumatized person to make sense of what has happened.

Preachers can help survivors by using varied vocal cadence, using some body movement, and potentially employing images for use during the sermon. Using a static projected image without words and not talking while the image is displayed allows the image to communicate. Visuals work better when preachers don't compete with them by preaching "over" them.

One way to avoid triggers for some survivors is for preachers to moderate their vocal tone so that they communicate the good news in higher, more playful cadences rather than using a tone that could register as anger.[18] This research corresponds to responses commonly given in preaching classes where student listeners reflect back to a classmate that they could not absorb meaning in a sermon because the tone was too harsh or loud.

Once the initial shock has been expressed, the move to clear, coherent language is essential for wounded people to heal. Van der Kolk puts communication in perspective: "Activists in the early campaign for AIDS awareness created a powerful slogan: 'Silence=Death.' Silence about trauma also leads to death—the death of the soul. Silence reinforces the godforsaken isolation of trauma."[19] Communication is crucial. Naming makes the experience real and validates survivors so that they can move toward healing.

However, a challenge in naming trauma is that the truth can sometimes put others off. Van der Kolk notes, "Being met by silence and incomprehension kills the spirit."[20] Polite conversation is not normally a place for painful truth-telling. At casual social gatherings, acquaintances may not want to hear about a returned soldier's traumatic experience or an abuse survivor's history. Survivors may want to speak, but no one wants to listen. This response from others leads to isolation for those with soul wounds.

Churches can support healing when they step into the space where others retreat. The incarnate Christ who continually casts his lot with broken humanity draws us toward each other by creating spaces where we can show ourselves, wounds and all. A climate of honesty and support contributes to the enormous success of groups like Alcoholics or Narcotics Anonymous.[21]

Preaching Tells the Hard Truth

Exposing dark secrets to the light of Christ can help remove the power of these deep wounds to control lives. Telling the truth in the pulpit about difficult parts of life creates a sense of trustworthiness for the preacher and deepens the relevance of preaching. When survivors hear their truth spoken from the pulpit, it legitimizes their experiences, humanizes them, and highlights their worth to God and the church. When the preacher admits that life is not perfect, it deepens our sense of need before God.

Fleming Rutledge is unparalleled in her unflinching honesty in the pulpit. Her view of the world is clear-eyed. Her sermons are deeply theological and truthful, both in their naming of pain and brokenness and in their Christ-centered hope. Her classic sermon, preached on Matthew's difficult text that details Herod's slaughter of children, "Monsters at the Manger," seeks to debunk the sentimental cultural drivel that dilutes the celebration of the Incarnation. She employs the hermeneutical tool of assigning blame with a sense of the powerful love of God. She also attends to survivors in her congregation by being careful with the language she uses to describe the horror of child abuse. She preaches,

> I took my mother to church on Christmas morning and we sang the familiar carols. My mother is a remarkable person, not afraid to ask the hard questions. We were driving home after the service, suddenly she said, "'Joy to the world, the Savior reigns.' What on earth does that mean? The Savior doesn't reign. Just look at all the horrible things that are going on...." In our reading today, we come up against the fact that, in the Christmas story as in today's world, the angels and monsters coexist.
>
> How can any readers of the newspapers believe in angels? Did you have the feeling that I did on December 29 when two of the most evil stories about child abuse ever to be seen in the *Times* appeared on the front page? I try to maintain an Ivan-Karamozov-like sense of unblinking outrage about life, but I confess those stories took me further into the sufferings of children than I wanted to go on the fifth day of Christmas. The details are much too ghastly to discuss here. Suffice it to say that the thought of a four-year-old boy being abducted, assaulted, and tortured for two whole days (imagine it!) and then hanged in a closet is a radical challenge to my faith. Where was that little boy's Savior during his indescribable ordeal? The mind reels and we turn away.
>
> If it were not for the Rachel passage, I believe that the claims of the Christmas story would be unendurable. In that case Baby Jesus and the angels and shepherds would have no more significance than Frosty the Snowman. This Christmas and every Christmas, the Rachel passage says to us that we can't run away from the suffering of the world. The suffering of the world is part of the story....
>
> I believe that, by putting Rachel's lament at the heart of the Christmas story, Matthew has shown us how to hold onto faith and hope until the Second Coming. Only as we share in the prayers and the laments of

bereaved families, not looking away, can we continue to believe that the Savior reigns even now in the faith and tenacity of...all those who continue to stand for humanity in the face of barbarity. Only by attending to the horrors of this world can we continue to sing the words of that great eighteenth-century hymn-writer Isaac Watts:

He comes to make his blessings known

Far as the curse is found. (Hymn, "Joy to the World")

For only a faith forged out of suffering can say that the angels and monsters will not coexist forever,...that the agonies of the victims will some day be rectified, and that the unconditional love of God in Jesus Christ will be the Last Word.[22]

Rutledge speaks the truth about our world and validates the experiences of those who have suffered wounds and abuse. She dares to speak the unspeakable—in church no less! The faith that she engenders in listeners is a complex faith that knows the limits and promise of humanity and offers hope grounded in Jesus Christ.

Hopeful but Imperfect Sermon Endings Help Listeners Identify God in Our World

For long-term healing of traumatic soul wounds, our journey may be one of integration rather than ultimate closure.[23] Healing may be partial on this side of God's realm. As preachers, our sermons can reflect this experience by avoiding too-tidy resolutions to the trouble in our sermons. Certainly we should not dial-down a truly miraculous experience, but we also shouldn't stretch to create seamless closure. In my sermon about the Hebrew midwives from Exodus 2, I clearly name Pharaoh's efforts at genocide in the text. Making a connection to our world, I recount the story of one woman's experience during the rule of the Khmer Rouge in Cambodia. My sermon theme was "God magnifies small actions." Rather than try to resolve the atrocities of war and genocide, I named the power of God in small acts that restored humanity in an inhumane context.

Phaly notices the other women who have survived are listless and dull-eyed—lying in their tents all day.

No one is caring for their own children, no one is bathing and caring for themselves.

These women were suffocating in a thick cloak of misery and despair. They no longer acted like people.

Phaly is filled with passion and compassion for these women.

She wants them to be able to see past the torture.

She wants them to feel useful again.

And so she thinks of one small act that she can do.

She comes alongside them as a midwife of hope.

She gathers the women in her tent and teaches them to give manicures and pedicures.

Gently handling fingers and toes, feeling their own humanity through the hands of others, these women began to feel alive again.

They are people with agency and power.

Through love, new skills, and gentle touch the cloak of despair is lifted and their tattered psyches slowly stitched together.

They are able to care for their families again.

As these women begin to care for their families, Phaly realizes that there are many orphans in the camp whose parents have not survived.

Together she and these formerly depressed women found Future Light Orphanage, which becomes the largest orphanage in Phnom Penh.[24]

God's action is present in the good news of the beginning of healing for these women, but the resolution is not perfect.

Preaching Defies the Gravity of a Wounding World

In *The Redress of Poetry,* Seamus Heaney pulls from the work of Simone Weil calling poets to write as a "counterweight" to the pain and injustice of the world.[25] Weil writes, "Obedience to the force of gravity. The greatest sin."[26] Heaney insists that artists have great responsibility in the face of "social wrong."[27] While still being very much earthbound and grounded discourse, preaching is also called to "defy gravity" by lifting our perspective to God's presence in the world that attends to the brokenhearted, heals the wounded, and raises the downcast. Much like the poetry of which Heaney writes, faithful preaching places "a counter-reality in the scales—a reality which can be only imagined but which nevertheless has weight because it is imagined within the gravitational pull of the actual and can therefore hold its own and balance out against the historical situation."[28] Preaching bears witness to the ongoing revelation of God in our world in ways that participate in God's healing in a reflective way, much like a mirror captures the light of the sun. What Heaney says about poetry can also be said of preaching:

> The redressing effect of poetry comes from its being a glimpsed alternative, a revelation of potential that is denied or constantly threatened by circumstances. And sometimes, of course, it happens that such a revelation, once enshrined in the poem, remains as a standard for the poet, so that he or she must then submit to the strain of bearing witness in his or her own life to the plane of consciousness established in the poem.[29]

Much like poetry, preaching can address the causes of soul wounds directly—naming evil for what it is in plain language. To hear that death is a thief; that war leads to pain, loss, and destruction rather than to God's peace; or that abuse of any kind leaves deep and lingering scars confirms the experiences of wounded listeners. Also like poetry, preaching can generate or utilize images, metaphors, or symbols that open up new worlds of possibility for listeners.

In his 2012 Advent sermon following the Sandy Hook school shooting, Robert Howard names the horror of the pain and shock of the tragedy and then turns to the heart of the gospel to offer a counterbalance to the horrific loss of children and school staff. In addition to making strong claims about the power of Christ that is stronger than death by preaching the cross and resurrection, he also turns to the Bible to provide language for our faith.

> Sisters and brothers, I tell you true: Jesus Christ came into this world of violence and grief, precisely to show us God's way. Didn't wait until things had calmed down. Came here, marched right up to violence and said, "Do your worst...you cannot win!" Death sealed him in a stone-cold tomb,

brushed his hands off, and said, "that'll fix him." But with Easter's dawn, the light shined again....Stronger...brighter...."For love is strong as death, Passion fierce as the grave" (Song of Songs 8:6). "The light shined in the darkness"—and still does!—and the darkness cannot overcome it. You want to know the real "reason for the season"? You want to know the true meaning of Christmas? The light came into a world of darkness...and the light will overcome all darkness.[30]

Time and Reflection Impart Healing Wisdom

When some time has passed, the preacher can continue to speak to traumatic events with the added gifts of time and prayerful rumination. This may especially be the case with preaching that resonates with a preacher's own wounds. We need time for extended deliberation to bear witness to our own stories and show vulnerability in ways that are fruitful for healing in our sermons. In her book about writing that deals with profound loss and grief, Jessica Handler encourages her readers to write something that one's inner critic might ordinarily deem "'too' honest or sad or angry" and not reread that writing for a month.[31] After a month, she invites writers to revisit the piece and assess how they feel about it.[32] She cautions memoirists that just because something brings strong emotion during writing doesn't mean that will translate to the page for readers.[33] The same is true for preachers. We may find ourselves moved by memories or details that we have left out. We may find ourselves crying in the pulpit with listeners who were moved by our display of emotion rather than what we said. Handler's process requires time—more time than the average preacher may work ahead on sermons. However, taking time to prayerfully reflect on our own experiences is a spiritually wise practice for preaching and creates an emotionally safe space for preachers and listeners. When preachers offer some vulnerability in sermons, it creates a culture where others may also be willing to be vulnerable. Mutual vulnerability strengthens relationships and builds a sense of community that can be healing amidst the isolating wounds of trauma.

Nearly two decades after the death of his ten-year-old daughter from cancer, John Claypool preached a pastorally motivated sermon using a hermeneutic that focused on the power of God. His sermon was strengthened by reflection on his own wounding experience. In "What Can We Expect of God?" Claypool addresses the deep disappointment and anger that many feel toward God following a wounding event or experience.[34] Drawing from Isaiah 40:29-31 and other texts, Claypool asserts that God does intervene in human history as grace in times of great trouble, although we may not always be able to see it at first because we do not understand the ways of God. God says to us, " 'My ways are not your ways.' "[35] At times God intervenes "miraculously" to alter someone's circumstances, just as Jesus did for the leper crying out for help in Mark's Gospel. This is the kind of intervention that we "instinctively" pray for. Claypool says that no one should feel bad or guilty for turning to God when life is at its worst. "Nobody in this room should feel guilty if, when you are really up against it, you lift your eyes to heaven and hope against hope that somehow energies from that realm will break into your realm and do something about your difficulty. It's the first instinct all of us have in a tight place."[36] He has already noted that Jesus himself calls out to God in the garden of Gethsemane.[37] Besides that which we would name as miraculous, Claypool names experiences of divine and human collaboration as a form of God intervening in our world. Biblically we see this in the role of Moses leading Israel out of slavery.[38] Claypool names cleaning up our environment and prayers for peace as being opportunities where God may be calling for human and divine collaboration.[39] The third pattern is an intervention of sustaining power. God offers strength to endure under horrific circumstances, which Claypool too names as a form of gracious intervention in our world.[40] Biblically this can be represented by the Apostle Paul's "thorn in the flesh."[41] In applying this form of intervention to our world, Claypool offers his own wounding experience of his daughter's illness and death. He recalls meeting a rabbi friend some weeks after his daughter's death.[42] His friend asks if God did anything for them in the midst of this horrific experience.[43] Claypool notes that they prayed for miraculous intervention and for God to collaborate with doctors and other medical experts, but the way that God intervened was to grant them the strength to endure.

> I could remember those times when I thought to my soul that I could not stand it for another minute. There was one day when they were trying to give her an injection. They could not find a working vein. They punched and punched and she cried in her agony and I thought to my soul, "I don't think I can stand it for another second." But the amazing thing is that somehow in the midst of the unspeakable, there was something that kept me from blowing up in anger or giving down in despair. I managed to stay there with her and for her, as did the whole family.
>
> And so, I was finally able to look my rabbi friend in the eye and say, "yes I've got to be honest with you: God did give us something, he gave us the power to endure what we could not change. He gave us the power to stay with something and instead of it defeating us and turning us bitter, somehow we were sustained by strength that was not our own. . . ."

Somebody has said that Isaiah has the sequence wrong, that first we walk, then we run, and then we soar with eagles. But those people have never been where I have been. They've never been in a hospital room with a little girl crying for all her heart's worth and realized that there is no occasion to soar, and no room to run. In those places the grace to walk and not faint is the very best gift in the world.[44]

Years of reflection gave John Claypool insights into his wounding experience and pastoral empathy with others carrying deep wounds. However, he doesn't mince words or try to "clean up" his experience, nor does he settle for easy answers or portray himself as an expert with all the answers. He speaks openly about his own experience and allows the mysterious ways of God to unfold.

Preaching through the Apostles' Creed Forms Listeners According to the Life of Christ[45]

Traumatic experience is powerful and life changing. While it certainly may impact identity, a survivor should not be reduced to a horrific event or events. Rather, this person is a brother or sister in Christ whose identity is in Christ and whose self and future are being transformed more and more into Christ's likeness. The ability to retell or reshape story and identity in the wake of trauma is an important part of psychological integration and healing. As Christians, we hold that through the waters of baptism, the Holy Spirit makes the identity of Jesus Christ definitive and constructive in shaping our own identities now and eschatologically. The events that helped form Jesus's earthly ministry are named in the christological section of the Apostles' Creed.

> I believe… [And] in Jesus Christ his only Son our Lord; who was conceived by the Holy Ghost, born of the Virgin Mary, suffered under Pontius Pilate, was crucified, dead, and buried; he descended into hell; the third day he rose again from the dead; he ascended into heaven, and sitteth on the right hand of God the Father Almighty; from thence he shall come to judge the quick and the dead.[46]

Preaching through the Apostles' Creed in a sermon series may offer preachers an approach to positively participating in the complex processes of healing soul wounds and building resilience. Preaching about the creed generates language and theology that may help rebuild and restore the identity of trauma survivors and form congregations in part through "typological identification" with aspects of Jesus's life and ministry.[47]

Oppressed and marginalized people have long drawn strength and hope from typological association.[48] Typology was used by exiles who recorded or redacted the stories of Abraham and Moses as a means of processing their experiences and naming God's provision and care in the midst of suffering. In America, enslaved Africans drew on the Exodus experience of Israel being freed from Egypt, while Puritan colonists who were seeking religious freedom connected to Israel being brought into the Promised Land.[49] Use of these key biblical images helped shape identity in ways that preserved and nurtured identity and calling in these groups. Typological association with Christ invites survivors to move beyond seeing themselves as "bystanders in a scene that also involves Christ" in order to nurture their Christian identity and "see in their own lives the stages that mark the history of Christ's ministry."[50]

In order to maximize typological connection, it is important to preach about the entirety of Jesus's life. While it is common practice in many ministry settings to move in and out of the Christian Year, a result can be unintentionally emphasizing some aspects of Christ's life and work and downplaying or ignoring others. However, since the journey to healing is multifaceted and different aspects of the Christ-event address different responses to trauma, each event in Jesus's life offers healing nuances.

"Conceived by the Holy Ghost, Born of the Virgin Mary": Preach Incarnation in Present Tense

God is deeply committed to creation and cares about what happens with human bodies in history. This is true throughout scripture but is most deeply marked by God entering into creation as a human. God's choice to become human in a sense elevates the value of humanity. Incarnation exemplifies God's desire to connect to people. Jesus's incarnation highlights the necessity of safety, relationship, and community. Preaching about these very human aspects of Jesus works against loss of self and isolation that many may feel following a traumatic event. In the immediate wake of trauma, the first step toward healing is the need for safety for the survivor. Safety needs to be both physical or external and internal or emotional/psychological. Safety was a concern for the infant Jesus as Mary sought a safe place to give birth. In Matthew's Gospel the family lived in Egypt to protect Jesus. The way that those with PTSD respond to physical stimuli and are unable to effectively employ self-soothing behaviors is in some ways reminiscent of a newborn infant. Identification or association with the infant Jesus, who is protected, honored, and loved, may be helpful.[51]

The role of Jesus's mother, Mary, and the fact that she was given a choice in Jesus's conception may be healing themes to lift up in Advent sermons. Judith Herman writes poignantly about the loss of self that can happen for those who experience trauma, particularly women who experience rape. She writes, "At the moment of trauma, almost by definition, the individual's point of view counts for nothing.... The traumatic event thus destroys the belief that one can be *oneself* in relation to others."[52] Jesus's ministry at times is characterized by being misunderstood in his closest relationships while also exhibiting a profound sense of understanding and compassion toward others.

In many contexts, it is common to preach about the "once for all-time" nature of Jesus's work. However, drawing from the strength of typological identification, it may encourage connection to not speak about Christ's incarnation as a "one-time event that happened in the distant past, but that ended with Christ's death on the cross."[53] Rather, identification with Christ may be encouraged by taking a different approach that, in Lynn Bridgers words, envisions "the incarnation as a rupture, as an eruption of God into the life of humanity whose impact is ongoing. The incarnation did not end with the cross but is continued in the lives of every believer today."[54] This might be fostered in preaching that uses present-tense verbs to talk about Jesus's incarnate presence and that consistently uses examples of believers acting as the present-day, incarnate body of Christ in our world.

"Suffered": Name Jesus's Presence in Situations of Suffering Today

Jesus's suffering may be one of the most theologically challenging elements in preaching, especially as it relates to involuntary human suffering today. Bridgers's comments concerning the eternal "eruption" of the incarnation of Christ may be helpful here as well. Indeed, while God has ultimately defeated death through the cross and resurrection, our world exists in an era of "overlap" where old life and new life exist together. Just as Jesus continues to be made incarnate, he may also be understood to still be suffering with and in people today. Nevertheless, preachers should be clear that Jesus's presence with those who suffer doesn't make their suffering a means to salvation or something that should be glorified in any way. However, a link with Christ's own suffering does provide a way to find meaning, some sense of purpose, and a way forward in what would otherwise feel like a hopeless situation. This may particularly be the case when preachers are consistent in linking the cross with the resurrection. These two events invade our world simultaneously, and we cannot speak of the cross without also engaging with the resurrection.[55] Jesus, who suffers wherever there is suffering today, is also the Risen Lord and is intimately involved in raising new life in our world.

Besides links with cross and resurrection, survivors often speak anecdotally of feeling Christ's presence with them in experiences of intense suffering. Naming Jesus's presence and solidarity with suffering people is a powerful word to counter the isolation and sense of separation that many survivors either experience based on others' discomfort or impose on themselves out of fear. Preaching that people are never alone in their experiences of suffering is an important word of comfort and hope.

"Was Crucified, Dead, and Buried": Incorporate Testimony to Shape Stories

A close brush with one's own physical death or the death of a loved one is part of the wound of trauma. In situations of terror people seek out elemental sources of "comfort and protection."[56] "Wounded soldiers and raped women cry for their mothers or for God. When this cry is not answered, the sense of basic trust is shattered. Traumatized people feel utterly abandoned, utterly alone, cast out of the human and divine systems of care and protection that sustain life.... They belong more to the dead than to the living."[57] Jesus's own cry, "My God, my God, why have you forsaken me," resonates with this experience and testifies to the gospel promise that God hears those cries and ultimately acts. Following the establishment of bodily safety and safe relationships, the second phase of recovery from trauma named by Herman is "remembrance and mourning." This is essentially the reclaiming and telling of the traumatic experience or memory so that it might be integrated into an emerging way forward.[58] Because much of traumatic memory and experience is stored in the brain without words, speaking the story and shaping it is transformative for survivors, in part because it tells the truth of what happened and allows them to become whole people.[59] Herman writes, "In the telling the trauma story becomes testimony.... Testimony has both a private dimension, which is confessional and spiritual and a public aspect, which is political and judicial."[60] In telling the story, the survivor moves from "shame and humiliation" to "dignity and virtue."[61] They "regain the world they have lost."[62] Creating appropriate time for testimony and allowing testimony to become part of the preaching moment may be a way for pastors to reach out to survivors. The survivor must take the lead, but the preacher will also want to be aware of the situation and the appropriateness of the testimony. Preaching that touches the complexity of atonement will want to not only build identification but also show that Jesus's actions have a vicarious power. Jesus takes on the horror for us so that we don't have to bear it alone. Jesus's death also brings a finality that can be life-giving, in particular for those with PTSD who experience aspects of the traumatic event again and again without a sense of ending or finality.[63] Survivors can send their experiences to the cross with Jesus and let them end once and for all. Inviting participants to write on a paper or bring forward a symbol to place on the cross may even be a helpful worship ritual for a Good Friday service. Integrating celebration of Communion with themes from the sermon may offer a helpful way for worshippers to experience Jesus's self-giving presence physically in ways that are beneficial when pain and brokenness are beyond words.

Rehearsing the death and resurrection of Jesus in a way that allows for deep identification offers potential healing for survivors of trauma. When the reliving of the traumatic experience is able to end, the memory changes, and the psychological response changes as the survivor is able to move forward again in new life.[64] However, ritual action and accompanying proclamation rarely address the questions of "why" and "why me" that follow integration of the trauma experience.[65] Here Bridgers again suggests that the life of Jesus is helpful, although the perspective of Jesus's followers may be more relatable than Jesus himself. Jesus's disciples did not understand the promise of the Resurrection until it happened. Our human perspective has limitations, and it can be beneficial for preachers to acknowledge these unknowns. It is not a cop-out to acknowledge mystery; rather, it affirms our creaturely relationship to God.

"He Descended into Hell": Name Pain in the Presence of God

Holy Saturday passes quietly in many traditions, but this time between Christ's death and resurrection where Jesus "harrows hell" may serve as a theological holding space for trauma survivors who may also feel caught in the middle between the past and the future, between life and death.[66] Trauma survivors may see their own journeys as a kind of descent into hell—a place of torment where others cannot reach and from where there is no return. Part of Jesus's redeeming act is to reach into hell—to reach beyond where humans can reach and return. Jesus is not limited, even in his death. Jesus is Lord of the dead and the living.[67] Preaching the descent into hell may take the form of pure lament, directed to a God who is present and listening, like in the tradition of the Psalms. James Kay brings in

Jewish understandings of Sheol as a place of the dead—where they exist as "shadows" cut off both from the world of the living and "oblivious to (the praise of) God."[68] This sounds like an apt description of those who are suffering the isolation of PTSD. Early commentators on the Apostles' Creed describe Jesus's actions in hell as involving proclamation and liberation where the good news is preached and the damned are set free from the chains and prisons that have held them.[69] Thus the first taste of resurrection is offered to those who are dead and enslaved. Christ's descent into hell is the transitional move from cross to resurrection.[70] This is profound good news for any who have been to "hell."

Preaching Christ's descent into hell may be particularly helpful for ministering to those who suffer because of violence they have committed against others, those who are guilty of crimes, or those who may have killed enemy combatants or innocent civilians in the context of war. Some may suffer from Perpetrator Induced Traumatic Syndrome (PITS) due to the honest and justifiable guilt they may experience from past actions. When he descends to hell, Jesus takes on the punishment reserved for the worst of the worst.[71] He takes his ranks among them. In Kay's words,

> Here we stand before an incomprehensible mystery where the Father and the Son, joined by a mutual Spirit of love and freedom, take into the very dynamics of their relationship the ravages of sin in order to destroy its dominance over the human creature.... Divine power is now seen as that which comes all the way down in suffering love to the depths of depravity and estrangement to bring forth eternal life. By descending into hell, God in the person of Jesus Christ places the worst that can befall human beings within the redeeming embrace of the cross.[72]

Some congregations have special worship services for recently released sex offenders. Conditions of release often do not permit them to worship in traditional church settings. I am most familiar with Dismas Fellowship services. My husband and I volunteered with Dismas Fellowship through a congregation where my husband served as pastor. Dismas Fellowship or similar services may feel controversial for congregations because of concern for crime victims. These services can also stir up unhealed wounds for some trauma survivors in the congregation. Preaching Jesus's descent into hell may be a helpful way for a pastor to work through the theological rationale for a program like this with a congregation as part of discernment around pursuing this ministry.

Finally, treatment and healing from trauma take time. The journey is long. Marking Christ's descent into hell and the "middle time" of Holy

Saturday acknowledges that the move from death to new life may be slow and painful. Preachers may want to mark this day in a way to slow the congregation down in the "rush" to get from Good Friday to Easter.[73] For family members and friends who accompany survivors on their journey, Christ's descent into hell offers assurance that Christ's power extends beyond the earthly and heavenly realms to those who are unable to respond and seem beyond reach and beyond hope.[74]

"He Rose again from the Dead": Preach about Transformation and New Life

Literature related to trauma and recovery often mentions the possibility of new life or a new start in the aftermath of wounding experiences. People describe survivors as having been deeply changed by their experiences. "John was a different person when he returned from Iraq," for example. Allowing the paradigm of Jesus's resurrection to offer narrative and formative structure to impact the way a survivor talks about his or her experience may be healing.[75] Theologically framing resurrection as not only an event that happened to Jesus long ago but as an eschatological event that has ongoing implications for creation may offer hope to survivors who must repeatedly choose life over death as they slowly move toward healing.

Survivors and their families may eventually embrace language that is reminiscent of the language the church uses to talk about death and resurrection. However, this perspective takes time, and it cannot be forced on a survivor. Many find healing and purpose in allowing the traumatic experience to become a "gift" to others, part of a sense of mission or calling in the world.[76] When a person successfully works through her or his experience, she or he may desire to share about it, and the sermon may be a space where this can happen.

"He Ascended into Heaven and Sitteth on the Right Hand of God the Father Almighty": Incorporate Body Awareness into Worship

The doctrine of Ascension is not often addressed or engaged in preaching, but when held together with the fullness of Christ's identity and work it offers nuances that may be helpful. Part of the healing process for some trauma survivors is finding a sense of containment for the traumatic experience.[77] They need to find ways to leave it behind so that it doesn't leak in and contaminate all parts of life. Van der Kolk suggests guided meditation where people are led in actions of body awareness and in creating physical "islands of safety"—that is, places in their body that feel safe in the midst of a triggering event.[78] For example, if breathing is becoming rapid and shallow, focusing on another body part, such as the hands, may help survivors be aware of themselves in the present moment to keep from moving into the past of a traumatic flashback.[79] Moments of body awareness can be integrated into prayers and other aspects of worship. In some traditions, individual and communal body awareness is also part of participation in the preaching moment. African American preachers often encourage these body-aware moments in the midst of preaching, saying "turn to your neighbor and say 'Jesus loves you!'" or inviting members to hold the hand or touch the shoulder of a neighbor.

When Jesus ascends to heaven, he does so as the Crucified and Risen Lord. The experience of the cross has been integrated into his identity, but he is not bound by it. The cross remains contained while Jesus is free and sovereign. Worship itself can also become a communal act that defeats isolation and a holding space where participants can name the grief and loss associated with trauma and move liturgically toward praise and acknowledgment of the life-preserving power of God made manifest in Jesus.[80] As Jesus is lifted up, so too our lives, experiences, and concerns are lifted up to God.

In the glory of Jesus's heavenly reign, we have a glimpse of our eschatological destiny. Jesus's ascension marks his promise and gift of the Holy Spirit who serves as comforter and advocate in the midst of trauma and the long, slow process of healing. Indeed, the Spirit is the one that empowers our own advocacy on behalf of those who may be suffering in ongoing situations of chronic abusive trauma. In Hunsinger's words, "We find comfort in the midst of affliction when we are reminded that the One who descends into every human hell we create and unwittingly or maliciously perpetuate is the very one who sits at the right hand of the Father in glory."[81]

"From Thence He Shall Come to Judge the Quick and the Dead": Preach about God's Justice

Many preachers struggle to preach about Jesus's second coming and the final judgment. However, for survivors who long for retribution and revenge, preaching Jesus's return may offer release as revenge and retribution are given over to God. The roots of much violence, both interpersonally and on a larger scale, may originate in unresolved pain and trauma. Unaddressed traumatic soul wounds may cause survivors to "act out" on others or "act in," harming themselves. For those who have unanswered questions and who have experienced the profound injustice of trauma (particularly chronic trauma caused by abuse over time) we can proclaim that Jesus will return and set things right. For those who have afflicted trauma on others, who suffer trauma from honest and earned guilt, Christ's coming judgment may be framed "cosmically" so that Jesus judges all that represents death and destruction.[82] All actions and experiences are subjected to the "universal victory of life over death."[83]

While many survivors may experience at least some measure of healing this side of the Eschaton, Jesus's return signals the final consummation of God's promises for healing for all of creation and ultimate restoration. When Jesus returns, every tear shall be dried, and the world will be made right.

Preaching through the christological portion of the Apostles' Creed offers a structured path for pastors to encourage typological association with Jesus. This connection to Jesus can support God's healing for people who suffer from a wide range of wounds and broken experiences, and contribute to broader Christian formation for the entire congregation in becoming more like Christ.

Strengthening the Church through Compassionate Witness

Compassionate witnesses are empowered by the Holy Spirit to move toward those who struggle with a variety of wounds. Their words and actions serve as signs of God's healing power and presence in the midst of wounding events and broken circumstances. Preaching that inspires compassionate witness not only supports resilience and healing but also strengthens the church as an important part of Christian formation.

Following a white supremacist rally that turned deadly in Charlottesville, Virginia, local residents struggled to make sense of what had happened and to feel a sense of connection and safety. My sister-in-law and nieces, who are Charlottesville natives, were especially upset about the setting of the downtown pedestrian mall, a place where they regularly went to a farmer's market, to restaurants, and to the children's museum. They felt that the place had been violated and were sad that a beautiful community gathering space had become associated with racism, fear, and death. After processing and brainstorming for a week after the demonstration, when all the media vehicles had gone, my sister-in-law took her Girl Scout troop to the downtown mall. A local florist donated flowers, which the girls handed out to shoppers, walkers, and storeowners on the mall that day. Their action restored connection between ordinary citizens and emphasized that the mall could again be a place of beauty. My sister-in-law's action is an example of the kind of compassionate witness described by Kaethe Weingarten.

Empathy is a key building block for compassionate witness but can often become entangled in a response of personal distress.[84] One of the biggest challenges of compassionate witness is to be present to the pain of another when a traumatic event may be upsetting to us.[85] For example, hearing another person's story may touch the wounds of a survivor of sexual assault. The survivor's resulting pain is often focused on his or her own experience. Weingarten carefully delineates how empathy is different from a response of personal distress. "Empathy stays focused on the other's experience, while personal distress, caused by having an emotional reaction to another's experience, is focused on relieving one's own anxiety or discomfort."[86] In many ways compassionate witness is an inefficient path for relieving distress because it invites us to move toward pain in order to stand with the other.[87] While it may be easier to note differences between personal distress and empathy on paper, in our lives it is much harder.

An initial sense of personal distress may transform into empathy. About eighteen months after my sister-in-law Twila's sudden death, my in-laws heard about the tragic death of one of their neighbors, a young farmer. At this stage of healing, the sudden death of any young person was an emotional trigger for my in-laws. Yet despite their personal distress, they reached out to their neighbors by showing up at his grief-stricken parents' home on a Sunday evening with a fresh-baked pie and an invitation to talk. That first overture was reciprocated several weeks later when the parents showed up at my in-laws with another pie and a desire to connect.

Preachers cannot pretend to be dispassionate when common shock strikes close to us. When we are aware of our own distress around an event, naming our involvement and connection can help our listeners understand where we are coming from. Preaching itself becomes a moment of compassionate witness when we name the pain and brokenness, and offer examples of God's incremental grace and healing in the midst of loss and tragedy.

When preaching from Ecclesiastes 2:12-23, pastor Serena Wolfe found herself resonating with Qoheleth's feelings of meaninglessness in the wake of an unresolved medical crisis involving a close friend.[88]

> I would love to say that Jared's story is an extreme, or something that rarely happens. Yet, as I think about the reality of our world, I cannot help but think that Jared's story is just another example in a long line of tales about fear or pain or suffering or death. Tales are shared about the loved

one who has overdosed one final time. Or of the woman who finds herself facing a life of loneliness after outliving her parents, siblings, and spouse. Or of yet another mass shooting that has claimed more young lives. We want to believe these are exceptions to this life, but the truth is nothing in this world stays the same for long and death eventually comes for us all.

And when we face change or death, all the things we value, all the things we have held tightly in life suddenly slip through our hands and we are left empty. Frustrated. We throw our hands up in anger and despair. Everything is meaningless.[89]

By including her experience, Wolfe normalized human responses to a range of crises and named her own pain and struggle with meaninglessness into the life of God and the church. Using the language of the Teacher in the text—"Everything is meaningless"—builds resonance between the text and our own wounding experiences. By placing herself alongside those struggling with faith, she can say tough words as one who struggles rather than one who has figured things out.

Beyond establishing credibility for the preacher as one who also struggles, preaching can participate in and amplify Spirit-fueled compassionate witness by sharing redemptive stories of how people respond to common shock in our world. Preaching and worship can also be acts of compassionate witness when preachers and other leaders place that intention on their words and actions. Finally, in the aftermath of common shock, preaching can suggest actions of response both concrete and symbolic, which can help foster healing and resilience.

Following the June 2015 shooting at Emanuel AME Church in Charleston, South Carolina, which killed nine church members including the pastor of the church who had gathered for a Wednesday evening Bible study, pastor Robert Howard's sermon responded to common shock by engaging directly with the event. Through his sermon, he shared the witness of surviving family members who offered forgiveness to shooter Dylann Roof.[90] He quotes family members offering God's forgiveness and asking God to show the shooter mercy. He draws a direct connection between these actions and biblical formation.[91] Throughout the sermon, he names biblical formation as a path toward resilience in the face of traumatic violence, using biblical language as the language of faith to offer comfort and to deepen the very formation he is seeking to promote and foster in his congregation. Howard also gives concrete suggestions for how the members of his congregation might respond. He preaches,

> So what can we do? Well, our first step is to follow Jeremiah's example: "For the hurt of my poor people I am hurt, I mourn, and dismay has

taken hold of me....O that my head were a spring of water, and my eyes
a fountain of tears, so that I might weep day and night for the slain of my
poor people!" (8:21; 9:1). As Paul recommended to the church in Rome,
we will "weep with those who weep" (12:15). There is a solidarity of tears,
in which "deep calls unto deep" (Psalm 42:7). We will voluntarily enter
into a ministry of suffering, following our Lord, whose eyes also knew the
sting of tears (John 11:35). And then, like Him, we will get busy trying
to "overcome evil with good" (12:21). Professor Juan Cole recommends
donating to the Emanuel African Episcopal Methodist Church. You can
use the website to do so easily.[92] What else can we do? We can pray for the
victims, for their families, for the shooter and his family. We can pray for
the persecutors, that they may be healed of their hate. And we can work
to remove all suspicion, any prejudice that comes our way. In the name
of Jesus Christ, we can oppose any form of racism. If you hear it wherever you are, call it out. Gently, lovingly. But call it out. For, as Malachi
protested, "Have we not all one father? Has not one God created us?"
(2:10). In our Vacation Bible School this week we will meet children we
do not know today. They are gifts from God. We will have the priceless
chance to bend them toward the light—and perhaps prevent another act
of violence years before it would happen. This is not just fun we will be
doing, friends—it is holy work. You, and I, and everyone who helps will
be busy mending the world. We will be creating a new future. We will be
listening to that letter from God.

Howard's sermon offers an outlet for dealing with common shock that nurtures healing, resilience, and Christian formation.

In his sermon following Michael Brown's murder, Otis Moss III clearly
names the reality of racism facing African Americans: "On a daily basis, we
witness our own lynching; but we witness micro-lynchings every day. If you
are a person of color and you are relatively conscious, you will find yourself
witnessing the micro-lynching of your own soul just living in America."[93] In
the same sermon, he employs the tool of blaming God and implicates the
church as he recounts the cries of those protesting in the streets of Ferguson,
Missouri: "The question that they were raising is where is God in all of this?
Where is the church? Where have the leaders gone? Our institutions have
failed us."[94] He builds the sermon to offer concrete responses to both the
common shock of the violence and unrest in Ferguson as well as the ongoing
traumatic wounds of racism. He preaches, "Police misconduct and accountability can be transformed only when we recognize that it is *our* problem. If
you relegate it to just one community, it's eventually in some form or fashion
going to visit your community. We need to see that we are all interconnected

and that we are connected together; this can only happen when this ethic to stand up for the vulnerable, this sacred mandate, operates within our soul."[95]

Conclusions

Those with deep wounds long to hear good news that tells the truth about human experience and meets them in the midst of pain and struggle. Preachers can communicate and promote God's care and healing for people with soul wounds. Sermons can normalize human responses to traumatic experiences move congregations to healing action, and cultivate resilience while attending to the immediate effects of wounding experiences of all kinds. Over time this preaching serves as a means of Christian formation grounded in the identity of Jesus Christ, which strengthens the church for the work of compassionate witness in a wounded world.

An experience of trauma or walking alongside those who have experienced trauma leaves little doubt about the devastating power of hopelessness. Hopelessness can also affect people who have smaller and less severe wounds accumulating in their souls. Hopelessness tells us many lies: that we are alone, that no one cares, that God has forsaken us, that life does not matter, and that things will never change.

However, the truth is that hope is more powerful than hopelessness. As preachers we are called to bear witness and to proclaim the hope of the gospel—that we are beloved, that God is always with us, that people care, that life is a gift, and that God is making all things new. In the words of Lamentations 3:19-23,

> The memory of my suffering and homelessness is bitterness and poison.
> I can't help but remember and am depressed.
> I call all this to mind—therefore, I will wait.
> Certainly the faithful love of the LORD hasn't ended;
> certainly God's compassion isn't through!
> They are renewed every morning.
> Great is your faithfulness.

While scars may remain, new gifts and capacity can grow in the aftermath of trauma and other experiences of loss and brokenness. In fact, while present-day practice treats those who have survived trauma as patients who need treatment in order to fully re-engage with community, in ancient cultures those who survived trauma often became spiritual leaders in their communities.[96] They were the ones who taught and cared for "normal people" because their suffering and survival gave them great insight into the depths of human experience.[97] This logic resonates with Jesus's own traumatic crucifixion and death at the heart of Christianity. God's own suffering in Christ means that even the most painful aspects of being human are drawn into the life of God and can be redeemed and transformed for the glory of God.

Kaethe Weingarten tells a story about hope and healing after trauma. Steve Biko was a prominent young anti-apartheid activist killed in police custody. Friends and family gathered more than two decades later to celebrate the wedding of Biko's son. A friend and executive director of the community development organization Steve Biko Foundation, Dr. Xolela Mangcu, experienced agonized internal questioning as he held together past trauma and present hope-filled events, watching his young daughter participate in the wedding as a "confetti girl."

> For his seven year-old-daughter the wedding, and her part in it, was simply the best day of her life. For Dr. Mangcu the day was rich and loaded with memory and meaning. He remembered Nkosinathi's cry, "The whites have killed my father," even as now, he admired the young man in his wedding suit....Archbishop Desmond Tutu, who spoke at the wedding, addressed his internal question. Tutu thanked Steve Biko for his son, who "through his marriage made it possible for us to celebrate with tears of joy, and become ordinary again."[98]

For Dr. Mangcu, "becoming ordinary" meant allowing his daughter to have her joy in that moment without making her revisit the communal wound of apartheid.

Life's ordinary and extraordinary moments exist together; this is part of God's gift of healing.[99] Now nearing the second anniversary of Twila's sudden death, my family too experiences the grace of the ordinary. We can joke and laugh at family gatherings, and it has become normal to talk about meeting at "Paul's house" instead of "Twila and Paul's" house. The children/grandchildren are growing, and we are planning to sit for family pictures, our first without Twila. My mother-in-law and father-in-law exhibit a stronger faith and voice thankfulness for the presence of their church community, family, and loved ones. Their thankfulness and healing is not static as it has also given them courage to reach out to others who have experienced traumatic loss.

Writing this book has brought purpose and God's healing to my experience with trauma. My hope is that readers will be informed, equipped, and encouraged to embrace God's healing for painful and wounding experiences in their preaching ministry. Restoration, healing, and the event of proclamation occur in a holy space opened up by the life-giving power of the Spirit, a space pregnant with possibility and hope. God promises us that trauma is "not the last word."[100] Jesus Christ has ultimately overcome death and the forces of death that drain life and meaning. Upon Christ's final return, the rupture between the Realm of God and our world will finally be healed. God will make God's home among people—wiping away tears and bringing joy and peace.[101]

Appendix A

Preaching when the Church Has Contributed to Wounds

Strategies	Application
Listen	• Avoid excuses or simplistic response. • Ask about triggers. • Give advanced notice.
Care	• Use stories and examples without stereotypes or easy answers. • Use true stories that have been widely published, protect anonymity, or use with permission. • Take collaborative approaches to Bible study and proclamation. • Incorporate testimony. • Express our limitations in the sermon.

Confess and Apologize	• Seek support of local or broader leadership. • Name previous denominational apologies and reparation as avenues for God's healing. • Avoid scapegoating.
Embrace nontraditional preaching space and metaphors for God	• Post or broadcast sermons online. • Vary metaphors for God. • Remember that gendered language may trigger some. • Consider alternative Communion liturgies.
Preach about justice	• Remind survivors that the wound is not their fault, wounding action was wrong, and God loves them. • Name institutional failure as trouble in our world. • Place forgiveness in God's hands. • Speak up for victims. • Support events for healing that occur outside of worship. • Focus on God's liberation from past experiences. • Encourage survivors to forgive themselves.
Uproot secrets and shame	• Name church-related wounds to remove stigma and isolation. • Use narrative and details to invite listeners into the world of the wounded. • Name God's grace and healing in fragmentary ways to show that process can be slow.

Avoid violence and stereotyping	<ul><li>Avoid profanity and violent details that can hijack the sermon.</li><li>Avoid us vs. them narratives and caricatures.</li><li>Test materials with a trusted group before preaching.</li><li>Consider a trigger warning in the bulletin the week before or on the church Facebook page.</li></ul>
Name grief	<ul><li>Attend to diverse perspectives.</li><li>Consider inviting an informed guest preacher.</li><li>Consider pulpit exchange with a community representing a different perspective.</li></ul>

A Trauma-Sensitive Exegetical Supplement

Trauma-Sensitive Preaching from Text to Sermon

These steps can supplement a broader method of sermon-creation.

1. Name what troubles us in and around the text.

2. Describe the structure, movement, and plot of the text.

3. Apply trauma-sensitive interpretive tools.

Tools	Sermon Application	
Scripture as language of faith	• Use direct scriptural quotations in the sermon. • Put biblical words in the mouths of • present-day-figures.	
Assigning of blame	Blaming God • Name this as a normal and biblical response to trauma. • Maintain relationship with God. • Signal a strong belief in the power of God. • Call upon God to act to hold to God's promises.	Blaming Self • Name this as a normal and biblical response to trauma. • Move listeners toward releasing our action or inaction into God's care.
Focus on the power of God	• Name God's action in the text. • Link God's power with God's love. • Name the history of texts with connection to trauma to help listeners understand characterization of God. • Name God's provision in our world in varied ways. • Avoid solutions that seem too easy or too tidy.	
Typology	• Use biblical figures to stand in for us and the troubles we experience today. • Use Jesus to stand in for us in a way that leads to redemption (see also sermon series on Apostles' Creed). • Make typological link to celebration of Communion.	
Cross and Resurrection	• Place the Cross and Resurrection in conversation with wounds in the text and our world. • Ask, what does the Crucified and Risen Jesus say to those who are hurting?	

Suggestions for Sermon Creation and Structure

- In the immediate aftermath of a traumatic event, be flexible: preaching to the moment is more important than a perfect sermon.

- For preaching about events that affect preachers personally, write sensitive parts of the sermon and wait several weeks before revisiting and preaching.

- Allow the gospel to counterbalance wounding experiences by ending the sermon with hope.

- Make sermon endings hopeful but not perfect, easy, or too tidy.

Suggestions for Sermon Illustrations

- Put stories in your own words to shape them according to needs of context.

- Tell stories of compassionate witness.

- Share stories of survivors *with permission*.

- Offer stories of reasonable/humble/incremental hope.

- Consider stories that humanize perpetrators.

Suggestions for Preaching Performance

- Use varied vocal cadence, consider singing.

- Raise pitch of voice.

- Use images.

- Utilize movement and invite listeners to move, turn to neighbor, etc.

Notes

1. Soul Wounds

1. Peter Levine, *Waking the Tiger: Healing Trauma* (Berkeley, CA: North Atlantic, 1997), 28.

2. Peter Bellini, Lecture, Work of Worship Class at United Theological Seminary, Dayton, OH, April 18, 2017.

3. Ibid.

4. Don Saliers, "The Bitter Christ: Suffering and Spirituality in Denial," *Spiritus: A Journal of Christian Spirituality* 10, no. 2 (Fall 2010): 295.

5. *STAR Strategies for Trauma Awareness and Resilience: Level 1 Participant Manual*, The Center for Justice and Peacebuilding, Eastern Mennonite University, Harrisonburg, VA, February 2018, 12.

6. Ibid.

7. Ibid., 15.

8. Ibid., 15.

9. Ibid., 14. Some have documented a PTSD-type response called Perpetrator Induced Traumatic Stress or PITS.

10. Brite Divinity School, "What Is Moral Injury?," April 5, 2018, https://brite.edu /programs/soul-repair/WhatisMoralInjury/.

11. *STAR*, 13.

12. Ibid.

13. Ibid.

14. Ibid., 13–14.

15. Ibid., 11.

16. Ibid., 15.

17. Paragraph from Joni Sancken, "When Our Words Fail Us," in *Theologies of the Gospel in Context*, ed. David Schnasa Jacobsen (Eugene, OR: Cascade, 2017), 120–21.

18. Paragraph from Sancken, "When Our Words Fail Us," 119. Information in this sentence from Carolyn Yoder, *The Little Book of Trauma Healing* (Intercourse, PA: Good, 2005), 6.

19. David J. Morris, *The Evil Hours: A Biography of Post-Traumatic Stress Disorder* (New York: Houghton Mifflin Harcourt, 2015), 13.

20. *STAR*, 11.

21. Ibid.

22. Ibid. See also Peter Levine, *Waking the Tiger*, 48–50.

23. *STAR*, 17. See also John Fawcett, ed., *Stress and Trauma Handbook: Strategies for Flourishing in Demanding Environments* (Monrovia, CA: World Vision Internationl, 2003), 24–26.

24. Ibid., 18–19.

25. Ibid., 19.

26. Ibid., 21–22.

27. Ibid., 22. Paragraph from Sancken, "When Our Words Fail Us," 121.

28. *STAR*, 20.

29. Ibid., 21.

30. Ibid.

31. Ibid.

32. Ibid., 22–23.

33. Ibid.

34. Ibid., 23. Paragraph from Sancken, "When Our Words Fail Us," 121–22.

35. *STAR*, 24–25.

36. Ibid., 27. See also Judith Herman, *Trauma and Recovery* (New York: Basic, 1992), 158. Paragraph from Sancken, "When Our Words Fail Us," 122.

37. Ibid., 30.

38. Ibid., 31.

39. Ibid.; David J. Morris, *The Evil Hours: A Biography of Post-Traumatic Stress Disorder* (New York: Houghton Mifflin Harcourt, 2015), 111.

40. Morris, *The Evil Hours,* 109.

41. Ibid.

42. Yoder, *The Little Book,* 31. Paragraph from Sancken, "When Our Words Fail Us," 122–23.

43. Deborah Van Deusen Hunsinger, *Bearing the Unbearable: Trauma, Gospel, and Pastoral Care* (Grand Rapids: Eerdmans, 2015), 7.

44. Ibid., 8.

45. Ibid.

46. Ibid. See also Serene Jones's call for restoration of agency as part of the healing process. Serene Jones, *Trauma and Grace* (Louisville: Westminster John Knox, 2009).

47. Hunsinger, *Bearing the Unbearable,* 8.

48. Ibid.

49. Ibid., 8–9.

50. Ibid., 9.

51. Ibid. See also James Gilligan, *Violence: Reflections on a National Epidemic* (New York: Random House, 1996), quoted in Howard Zehr, "Doing Justice Healing Trauma: The Role of Restorative Justice in Peacebuilding," *South Asian Journal of Peacebuilding* 1, no. 1 (Spring 2008): 5.

52. The Witnessing Project, "Whether We Like It or Not, Everyday, We Observe Disturbing Events," accessed August 16, 2017, http://www.witnessingproject.org/what-we-do.

53. Kaethe Weingarten, *Common Shock: Witnessing Violence Every Day* (New York: New American Library, 2003). See also Hunsinger, *Bearing the Unbearable,* 24.

54. Ibid.

55. The Witnessing Project, "About Kaethe Weingarten," http://www.witnessingproject.org/common-shock/about-kaethe-weingarten, accessed August 16, 2017.

56. Ibid.

57. Hunsinger, *Bearing the Unbearable,* 23.

58. Exod 34:6; Ps 78:38; Ps 103; Lam 3:22-23; Deut 13:17; 30:3; Isa 49:15.

59. Andrew Purves, *The Search for Compassion: Spirituality and Ministry* (Louisville: Westminster John Knox, 1989), 69.

60. Ibid.

61. Ibid.

62. Weingarten, *Common Shock*, 192–93. See also Hunsinger, *Bearing the Unbearable*, 25.
63. Chantal Da Silva, "Hockey Fans Leave Sticks on Porches to Honor Victims of Humboldt Broncos Crash," May 11, 2018, http://www.newsweek.com/americans-join-canadians-putting-hockey-sticks-out-their-porches-honor-878900.
64. CBC News, "Canadians Don Hockey Jerseys in Show of Solidarity with Humboldt," May 11, 2018, http://www.cbc.ca/news/canada/humboldt-bus-crash-jersey-day-social-media-1.4616226.
65. Hunsinger, *Bearing the Unbearable*, 40.
66. Kaethe Weingarten, "Reasonable Hope: Construct, Clinical Applications, and Supports," *Family Process* 49, no. 1 (2010). See also Hunsinger, *Bearing the Unbearable*, 33–34.
67. Weingarten, "Reasonable Hope," 7.
68. Ibid.
69. Hunsinger, *Bearing the Unbearable*, 38.
70. Weingarten, "Reasonable Hope," 8.
71. Hunsinger, *Bearing the Unbearable*, 34.
72. Weingarten, "Reasonable Hope," 10.
73. Ibid.
74. Ibid., 19.
75. Ibid., 16.
76. Kaethe Weingarten, "Stretching to Meet What's Given: Opportunities for a Spiritual Practice," in Froma Walsh, ed., *Spirituality in Families and Family Therapy* (New York: Guilford, 199), 12.
77. Ibid., 21.
78. Ibid.
79. My father-in-law has given permission to share his story.
80. Language of "God's signature" on the stories we use in our sermons comes from Paul Scott Wilson, Lectures, Summer Preaching Seminar at United Theological Seminary, Dayton, OH, August 9–11, 2017.
81. Hunsinger, *Bearing the Unbearable*, 34.
82. Weingarten, "Reasonable Hope," 15.
83. Ibid.
84. Ibid., 21.
85. Ibid., 15, 19, 21.
86. Ibid., 17–18.
87. Ibid., 18.
88. *STAR*, 18; World Bank, World Development Report 2011: Conflict, Security, and Development, https://openknowledge.worldbank.org/handle/10986/4389.
89. Ibid.
90. Ibid.
91. See also ibid.
92. Hunsinger, *Bearing the Unbearable*, 1.
93. Ibid., 6.
94. Ibid. See also Judith Herman, *Trauma and Recovery*, 43.
95. *STAR*, 17.
96. Ibid.
97. Hunsinger, *Bearing the Unbearable*, 10–11.
98. Ibid., 12–13.
99. Andrew Sung Park, *From Hurt to Healing: A Theology of the Wounded* (Nashville: Abingdon, 2004), 11.
100. Ibid., 10–14.

101. Andrew Park, *The Wounded Heart of God: The Asian Concept of Han and the Doctrine of Sin* (Nashville: Abingdon, 1993), 20–30.
102. Ibid., 31–32.
103. Ibid., 33.
104. Ibid., 34–35.
105. Ruth 1:20.
106. Ibid., 35.
107. Ibid., 36–40.
108. Park, *Hurt to Healing,* 16.
109. Ibid., 35.
110. Ibid.
111. Ibid., 38–44.
112. Ibid., 40–41.
113. Ibid., 41.
114. Ibid., 46–47, 72.
115. Ibid., 61.
116. Ibid., 103.
117. Ibid., 132.
118. Shelly Rambo, "Spirit and Trauma," *Interpretation* 69, no. 1 (January 2015): 13.
119. Ibid.
120. Ibid.
121. Ibid., 14.
122. Ibid., 15
123. Ibid., 16.
124. Ibid.
125. Ibid.
126. Ibid., 16–17.
127. Shelly Rambo, *Spirit and Trauma: A Theology of Remaining* (Louisville: Westminster John Knox, 2010), 119–20, 132.
128. Ibid., 122.
129. Ibid., 115.
130. Ibid., 126–27.
131. Ibid. See also Hans Urs Von Balthazar, *Mysterium Paschale: The Mystery of Easter,* trans. Aidan Nichols (Grand Rapids: Eerdmans, 1993), 173.
132. Ibid., 127. See also Flora Keshgegian, *Time for Hope: Practices for Living in Today's World* (New York: Continuum, 2006), 102, 113.
133. Rambo, *Spirit and Trauma,* 129. See also the introduction to Cornel West's essay, "Philosophical View of Easter," in *The Cornel West Reader* (New York: Basic Civitas, 1999), 415.
134. Rambo, *Spirit and Trauma,* 132.

2. Soul Wounds in the Bible

1. David Carr, "Lessons the Bible Teaches Us about Trauma," *OnFaith,* June 6, 2018, https://www.onfaith.co/onfaith/2015/05/12/5-lessons-the-bible-teaches-us-about-trauma/36832.
2. Anna Akhmatova, "Requiem," *Selected Poems,* trans. Richard McKane (London: Oxford University Press, 1969), 90. Discussed in Joni Sancken, "When Our Words Fail Us," in *Theologies of the Gospel in Context,* ed. David Schnasa Jacobsen (Eugene, OR: Cascade, 2017), 113.
3. David Carr, *Holy Resilience: The Bible's Traumatic Origins* (New Haven: Yale University Press), 69–70.

4. Ibid., 70.

5. Ibid., 71. Lam 5:20-22 (CEB).

6. Ps 137:1-6.

7. Carr, *Holy Resilience*, 73.

8. Ibid.

9. Ibid., 79.

10. Ibid., 80.

11. Ibid.

12. See also Kathleen M. O'Conner, "Stammering toward the Unsayable: Old Testament Theology, Trauma Theory, and Genesis," *Interpretation* 70, no. 3 (July 2016): 305.

13. Jer 4:19.

14. Jer 1:18.

15. O'Connor, "Stammering," 304.

16. Ps 89:39-49.

17. Carr, *Holy Resilience*, 26, 32.

18. Ibid., 33–34.

19. Ibid., 32–33.

20. Carr, *Holy Resilience*, 77.

21. Ibid., 78.

22. Ibid.

23. Carr, "Lessons the Bible Teaches."

24. Carr, *Holy Resilience*, 95–96.

25. O'Connor, "Stammering," 306. See also Carr, *Holy Resilience*, 95, 101.

26. O'Connor, "Stammering," 306.

27. Ibid., 312.

28. Ibid.

29. Ibid., 310.

30. Ibid.

31. Ibid.

32. Ibid.,308.

33. Ibid.

34. See also Carr, *Holy Resilience*, 101.

35. O'Connor, "Stammering," 310–11.

36. Carr, *Holy Resilience*, 101.

37. Ibid., 113–14.

38. Ibid., 114.

39. Ibid.

40. Ibid., 116; Exod 7:5; 8:22; 10:2; 14:4, 18.

41. Carr, *Holy Resilience*, 116.

42. Ibid., 117–18.

43. Ibid., 118.

44. Carr, *Holy Resilience*, 163–65.

45. Ibid., 167–68. Carr is drawing on the work of Ellen Aitken, *Jesus' Death in Early Christian Memory* (Göttingen, Germany: Vandenhoeck & Ruprecht, 2004), 69–71.

46. Ibid., 170.

47. Ibid.

48. Acts 9:3-9; Carr, *Holy Resilience*, 177.

49. Carr, *Holy Resilience*, 178–79.

50. Ibid., 180–81.

51. 2 Cor 12:7-10; Gal 4:13-14; Carr, *Holy Resilience*, 189.

52. 2 Cor 11:23-29.

53. See also Carr, *Holy Resilience,* 190.

54. Walter Brueggemann, *Genesis,* Interpretation (Atlanta: John Knox, 1982), 186.

55. Eugene F. Roop, *Genesis,* Believer's Church Commentary (Scottdale, PA: Harold, 1942), 146–47.

56. Jon Levenson, *Inheriting Abraham: The Legacy of the Patriarch in Judaism, Christianity, and Islam* (Princeton: Princeton University Press, 2012), 75.

57. Ibid., 75–76.

58. Brueggemann, *Genesis,* 188.

59. Ibid., 189.

60. Ibid., 191.

61. Roop, *Genesis,* 148.

62. Levenson, *Inheriting Abraham,* 79.

63. Ibid.

64. Roop, *Genesis,* 144.

65. Ibid., 145.

66. Ibid., 146.

67. Søren Kierkegaard, *Fear and Trembling* (New York: Penguin, 1985).

68. Immanuel Kant, *Religion and Rational Theology,* trans. and ed. Allen W. Wood and George Di Giovanni (Cambridge: Cambridge University Press, 1996), 283. From *The Conflict of the Faculties,* 7:63. See also Levenson, *Inheriting Abraham,* 106.

69. Levenson, *Inheriting Abraham,* 106.

70. Roop, *Genesis,* 149.

71. Ibid.

72. Brueggemann, *Genesis,* 191.

73. Ibid., 192–93.

74. Ibid., 150. See also *Ante-Nicene Fathers,* vols. I, III, IV.

75. Melito of Sardis, "On the Passover" paragraphs 9, 69.

76. Levenson, *Inheriting Abraham,* 101–3.

77. Roop, *Genesis,* 150.

78. Peter K. Stevenson and Stephen I. Wright, *Preaching the Atonement* (New York: T&T Clark, 2005), 8.

79. Ibid., 8–9.

80. Ibid., 10.

81. One can imagine that Hagar and Ishmael being sent away may have been wounding for Isaac as well.

82. Stevenson and Wright, *Preaching the Atonement,* 10–11.

83. Buttrick's sermon, as quoted in Richard L. Eslinger, *A New Hearing: Living Options in Homiletic Method* (Nashville: Abingdon, 1987), 168.

84. This is also the case with other significant losses.

85. Amy Winnie, "Genesis 22 Sermon," sermon, Preaching to Preach class, United Theological Seminary, Dayton, OH, June 29, 2017.

3. Soul Wounds in the Church

1. Carolyn Yoder, *The Little Book of Trauma Healing* (Intercourse, PA: Good, 2005), 52–53; Marie Fortune, *Sexual Violence: The Sin Revisited* (Pasadena, TX: Pilgrim, 2005), 186–87.

2. Hillary Jerome Scarsella, "Responding to Reports of Abuse: Who's Getting It Right? And Where Does Theology Come In?" January 26, 2018, http://www.ourstoriesuntold.com /responding-to-reports-of-abuse/.

3. Recent case in point in the media: Christina Zhoa, "Tennessee Pastor Gets Standing

Ovation after Admitting 'Sexual Incident' with Teen," January 10, 2018, http://www.news
week.com/andy-savage-megachurch-pastor-sexual-assault-standing-ovation-776646.

4. Yoder never contested the veracity of charges brought against him by church and seminary accountability and disciplinary groups. He defended his behavior. Formal legal charges
were never made. Rachel Waltner Goossen, "'Defanging the Beast': Mennonite Responses
to John Howard Yoder's Sexual Abuse," *The Mennonite Quarterly Review* 89, no. 1 (January
2015): 7–80.

5. Anabaptist Mennonite Biblical Seminary has revisited Yoder's abuse carefully and engaged with victim/survivors. They eventually held a weekend-long event and worship service
with public confession, apology, and worshipful lament. They have also created a policy for
teaching about Yoder. "AMBS Statement on Teaching and Scholarship Relating to John Howard Yoder," *Anabaptist Mennonite Biblical Seminary,* April 20, 2012, https://www.ambs.edu
/academics/teaching-scholarship-yoder.

6. Judith Herman, *Trauma and Recovery* (Philadelphia: Basic, 2015), 7.

7. Ibid.

8. Ibid., 7–8.

9. Ibid.

10. Ibid.

11. Ibid.

12. Ibid.

13. Ibid.

14. Ibid.

15. Maureen O'Hara and Aftab Omer, "Virtue and the Organizational Shadow: Exploring False Innocence and the Paradoxes of Power," in *Humanity's Dark Side: Evil, Destructive
Experience, and Psychotherapy*, ed. A. C. Bohart, B. S. Held, E. Mendelowitz, and K. J. Schnei-
der (Washington: American Psychological Association, 2013), 168.

16. Ibid., 167–87.

17. Ibid., 168.

18. Ibid., 179.

19. Ibid., 168.

20. Ibid., 173–74.

21. Ibid., 174.

22. Ibid., 175.

23. Ibid.

24. Ibid., 175–76.

25. Ibid., 177.

26. Ibid., 178.

27. Ibid., 184.

28. Fortune, *Sexual Violence*, 187–88.

29. Ibid., 188–89.

30. O'Hara and Omer, "Virtue," 182.

31. *STAR Strategies for Trauma Awareness and Resilience: Level 1 Participant Manual*,
The Center for Justice and Peacebuilding, Eastern Mennonite University, Harrisonburg, VA,
February 2018, 125.

32. Fortune, *Sexual Violence*, 128.

33. Ibid., 127.

34. Rom 8:26.

35. *STAR*, 93.

36. David E. Anderson, "Lutherans Apologize for Anabaptist Persecution," *The Christian
Century* 125, no. 16 (August 12, 2008): 16.

37. Links to relevant statements posted on AMBS website: "AMBS Response to Victims of John H. Yoder Abuse," *Anabaptist Mennonite Biblical Seminary*, March 21–22, 2015, https://www.ambs.edu/about/ambs-response-to-victims-of-yoder-abuse. See also "AMBS Holds Lament Service for Yoder Victims," *The Mennonite*, March 23, 2015, https://the mennonite.org/daily-news/ambs-holds-lament-service-for-yoder-victims/.

38. Sara Wenger Shenk, "The Year of the Lord's Favor," preached at Anabaptist Mennonite Biblical Seminary, https://www.ambs.edu/about/ambs-response-to-victims-of-yoder -abuse, sermon, Elkhart, IN, March 22, 2015; see also Anabaptist Mennonite Biblical Seminary, "The Year of the Lord's Favor," March 31, 2015, https://www.ambs.edu/publishing blog/715842/the-year-of-the-lord-s-favor.

39. Ibid.

40. Ibid.

41. Ibid.

42. Ibid.

43. See also O'Hara and Omer, "Virtue," 181.

44. Ibid., 181–82.

45. Hillary Jerome Scarsella, with Rhoda Keener, Eleanor Kreider, David B. Miller, and John Remple, "The Lord's Supper: A Ritual of Harm or Healing," *Leader* 13 no. 4 (Summer 2016): 37.

46. Fortune, *Sexual Violence*, 126.

47. Ibid., 159.

48. Ibid., 126.

49. Fortune, *Sexual Violence*, 126.

50. Nancy J. Ramsay, "Preaching to Survivors of Child Sexual Abuse," in *Preaching about Sexual and Domestic Violence*, ed. John S. McClure and Nancy J. Ramsay (Cleveland, OH: United Church Press, 1998), 61–63.

51. Herman, *Trauma and Recovery*, 178.

52. *STAR*, 91.

53. Ibid., 93.

54. Herman, *Trauma and Recovery*, 7–9.

55. O'Hara and Omer, "Virtue," 180.

56. Ibid.

57. Ibid.

58. Ibid., 181.

59. Ibid., 182–83.

60. Ibid., 183.

61. Ibid.

62. Ibid., 185.

63. Joni Sancken, "Defanging the Snakes," sermon, United Theological Seminary Chapel Service, March 7, 2018.

64. Tristan Hopper, "'Vicious' Python Kills Two Sleeping Children, Aged 5 and 7, after Escaping from N.B. Pet Store," May 31, 2018, http://nationalpost.com/news/canada/two -children-die-after-python-escapes-in-campbellton-n-b-reports.

65. Raymond Brown, *The Message of Numbers: Journey to the Promised Land* (Downers Grove, IL: InterVarsity, 2002), 17.

66. Anje Ackerman Cassel, "I, Anje," January 31, 2018, https://www.survivorsstanding tall.org/blog-1.

67. Andrew Park is a professor at United Theological Seminary, where this sermon was

preached. He introduces this idea in his book *From Hurt to Healing* (Nashville: Abingdon, 2004), 10–15.

68. Katherine Doob Sakenfeld, *Numbers: Journeying with God* (Grand Rapids: Eerdmans, 1995), 118.

69. The website includes a content warning on the homepage.

4. Healing for Wounded Souls

1. Paragraph paraphrased from Joni Sancken, "When Our Words Fail Us," in *Theologies of the Gospel in Context*, ed. David Schnasa Jacobsen (Eugene, OR: Cascade, 2017), 114–15.

2. Ibid., 155–56.

3. Ibid., 156.

4. Bessel van der Kolk, *The Body Keeps the Score* (New York: Penguin, 2014), 281.

5. *STAR Strategies for Trauma Awareness and Resilience: Level 1 Participant Manual*, The Center for Justice and Peacebuilding, Eastern Mennonite University, Harrisonburg, VA, February 2018, 120–21.

6. Ibid., 121.

7. Ibid., 122.

8. Ibid., 123.

9. Ibid.

10. Ibid., 125.

11. Ibid.

12. Ibid., 126.

13. Ibid., 127.

14. Van der Kolk, *Body Keeps the Score*, 43–44.

15. Ibid., 44.

16. Ibid., 44–45.

17. Ibid., 45.

18. Ibid., 88.

19. Van der Kolk, *Body Keeps the Score*, 234.

20. Ibid.

21. Ibid.

22. Fleming Rutledge, "Monsters at the Manger," in *The Bible and the New York Times* (Grand Rapids: Eerdmans, 1998), 57–60.

23. Jessica Handler, *Braving the Fire* (New York: St. Martin's, 2013), 211. See also Susan O'Doherty, *Getting Unstuck without Coming Unglued* (Berkeley, CA: Seal, 2007).

24. Joni Sancken, "Midwives of Hope," sermon, United Theological Seminary Deborah's Daughter's Conference, October 23, 2014. Phaly Nuon's story is told in Andrew Solomon, *The Noonday Demon: An Atlas of Depression* (New York: Scribner, 2001).

25. Seamus Heaney, *The Redress of Poetry* (New York: Farrar, Straus and Giroux, 1995), 3.

26. Ibid.; Simone Weil, *Gravity and Grace* (London: Routledge, 1963), 2–3.

27. Kaethe Weingarten, *Common Shock* (New York: New American Library, 2003), 188; see also Heaney, *Redress*, 5.

28. Heaney, *Redress*, 3–4.

29. Ibid., 4.

30. Robert Howard, "Sermon Following the Shootings in Newtown, CT," sermon, First Christian Church, Globe, AZ, December 16, 2012.

31. Handler, *Braving the Fire*, 188.

32. Ibid.

33. Ibid., 186.

34. John Claypool, "What Can We Expect of God?" in *This Incomplete One,* ed. Michael D. Bush (Grand Rapids: Eerdmans, 2006), 35–51.

35. Ibid., 37–38.

36. Ibid., 41.

37. Ibid.

38. Ibid., 42–43.

39. Ibid., 44.

40. Ibid., 45.

41. Ibid., 45–46.

42. Ibid., 47.

43. Ibid.

44. Ibid., 48–51.

45. The section Preaching through Apostles' Creed Forms Listeners According to Life of Christ is quoted from Sancken, "When Our Words Fail Us," 124–33.

46. I've chosen to use the "traditional" version rather than the Ecumenical version, which is likely used more frequently in worship because it includes the line, "he descended into hell." I see this element as being very important in light of the context of trauma and trauma survivors.

47. Lynn Bridgers, "The Resurrected Life: Roman Catholic Resources in Posttraumatic Pastoral Care," *International Journal of Practical Theology* 15, no. 1 (2011): 39.

48. Ibid., 43.

49. Ibid. See also Theophus H. Smith, *Conjuring Culture: Biblical Foundations of Black America* (New York: Oxford University Press, 1994), 55.

50. Bridgers, "Resurrected Life," 43.

51. Bessel A. van der Kolk, "In Terror's Grip: Healing the Ravages of Trauma," June 8, 2018, http://www.traumacenter.org/products/pdf_files/terrors_grip.pdf, 6–7.

52. Judith Herman, *Trauma and Recovery* (Philadelphia: Basic, 2015), 53.

53. Bridgers, "Resurrected Life," 43.

54. Ibid., 43–44. Bridgers comments on feminist concerns around women being able to identify with the male Jesus Christ, which has an exclusionary history of restricting women's authority. However, she sidesteps this concern by focusing on the form of Jesus's life. Along similar lines, I would argue for identification in Jesus's actions more than his specific gender identity.

55. See also Bridgers, "Resurrected Life," 45.

56. Ibid., 52.

57. Ibid.

58. Herman, *Trauma and Recovery,* 175.

59. Ibid., 175–81.

60. Ibid., 181.

61. Ibid. See also R. Mollica, "The Trauma Story: The Psychiatric Care of Refugee Survivors of Violence and Torture," in *Post-Traumatic Therapy and Victims of Violence,* ed. F. Ochberg (New York: Bruner/Mazel, 1988), 312.

62. Herman, *Trauma and Recovery,* 181.

63. Van der Kolk, "In Terror's Grip," 3–4.

64. Ibid., 5.

65. Herman, *Trauma and Recovery,* 178.

66. Shelly Rambo, "Saturday in New Orleans: Rethinking the Holy Spirit in the Aftermath of Trauma," *Sage Journals* 105, no. 2 (May 1, 2008): 231–32, https://doi.org/10.1177/003463730810500206.

67. See also James F. Kay, "He Descended into Hell," *Word & World* 31, no. 1 (Winter 2011): 23; Rom 14:9.

68. Kay, "He Descended," 20.

69. Ibid. Kay cites Rufinus, *A Commentary on the Apostles' Creed*, trans. and ed. J. N. D. Kelly (New York: Newman, 1978), 51–52, 61.

70. Kay, "He Descended," 23.

71. Ibid., 24.

72. Ibid.

73. Rambo, "Saturday in New Orleans," 234, citing Walter Brueggemann, "Readings from the Day 'In Between,'" in *A Shadow of Glory: Reading the New Testament after the Holocaust*, ed. Tod Linefelt (New York: Rutledge, 2002), 110–11.

74. See also Kay, "He Descended," 23–24.

75. Bridgers, "Resurrected Life," 42–43.

76. Ibid., 47.

77. Deborah Van Deusen Hunsinger, *Bearing the Unbearable: Trauma, Gospel, and Pastoral Care* (Grand Rapids: Eerdmans, 2015), 17.

78. Van der Kolk, *Body Keeps the Score*, 247.

79. Ibid.

80. Hunsinger, *Bearing the Unbearable*, 24; Bridgers, "Resurrected Life," 51.

81. Hunsinger, *Bearing the Unbearable*, 25.

82. Kay, "He Descended," 25.

83. Ibid.

84. Lenny Luchetti's book *Preaching with Empathy: Crafting Sermons in a Callous Culture* (Nashville: Abingdon, 2018) has suggestions for incorporating empathy into sermons.

85. Weingarten, *Common Shock*, 167.

86. Ibid.

87. Ibid.

88. Serena Wolfe, "Wisdom Sermon," sermon in class, Preaching Across the Bible, United Theological Seminary, Dayton, OH, February 28, 2018.

89. Ibid.

90. Robert Howard, "Message from a Father," sermon, First Christian Church, Globe, AZ, June 21, 2015; see also "In Charleston, Raw Emotion at Hearing for Suspect in Church Shooting," *The New York Times*, June 19, 2015, https://www.nytimes.com/2015/06/20/us/charleston-shooting-dylann-storm-roof.html?module=inline.

91. Ibid.

92. Juan Cole, "Our Reply to Dylann Roof's Hate: Donate to 'Mother Emanuel' AME Church," *Informed Comment Blog*, June 19, 2015, http://www.juancole.com/2015/06/donate-mother-emanuel.html.

93. Otis Moss III, "Ministry and Our Mandate," in *Blue Note Preaching in a Post-Soul World* (Louisville: Westminster John Knox, 2015), 96.

94. Ibid., 97.

95. Ibid., 99.

96. David J. Morris, *The Evil Hours: A Biography of Post-Traumatic Stress Disorder* (New York: Houghton Mifflin Harcourt, 2015), 65–66.

97. Ibid.

98. Weingarten, *Common Shock*, 241. See also Xolela Mangcu, "A Wedding Story," *South Africa Development Fund*, Fall 2001.

99. Ibid.

100. Serene Jones's phrasing. Shelly Rambo et al., "Theologians Engaging Trauma Transcript," *Theology Today* 68, no. 3 (October 2011): 227.

101. John Wesley's understanding of human healing and sanctification is that creation's ultimate restoration will be more glorious even than the pre-fallen creation of Eden. Randy Maddox, *Responsible Grace: John Wesley's Practical Theology* (Nashville: Kingswood, 1994), 62. See also John Wesley, Sermon 59, "God's Love to Fallen Man," *Works,* 2:423–35 and Sermon 60, "The General Deliverance," *Works,* 2:445–50. Portions of this paragraph from Joni Sancken, "When Our Words Fail Us," 137.

Printed in September 2023
by Rotomail Italia S.p.A., Vignate (MI) - Italy